Navegando 1

Program Manager
with Daily Lesson Plans

Angela M. Swedberg

EMCParadigm Publishing

Saint Paul, Minnesota

Product Manager
James F. Funston

Associate Editor
Alejandro Vargas Bonilla

ISBN: 0-8219-2807-4

Published by EMC/Paradigm Publishing
875 Montreal Way
St. Paul, Minnesota 55102
800-328-1452
www.emcp.com
E-mail: educate@emcp.com

Printed in the United States of America
1 2 3 4 5 6 7 8 9 10   XXX 09 08 07 06 05 04

Table of Contents

Introduction v

Regular Class Period (50 Minutes)

Capítulo 1 1

Capítulo 2 11

Capítulo 3 21

Capítulo 4 31

Capítulo 5 41

Capítulo 6 51

Capítulo 7 61

Capítulo 8 71

Capítulo 9 81

Capítulo 10 91

Block Schedule (90 Minutes)

Capítulo 1 95

Capítulo 2 104

Capítulo 3 113

Capítulo 4 122

Capítulo 5 131

Capítulo 6 141

Capítulo 7 150

Capítulo 8 159

Capítulo 9 168

Capítulo 10 177

Introduction

Teachers know that lesson planning can be difficult. Interruptions such as fire drills, pep assemblies and illness are just three examples of the many factors that affect instructional contact time and that require teachers to adjust their daily lesson plan. Furthermore, methodology, instructional time, philosophy and individual learner needs all vary greatly from one classroom to the next. Some schools offer traditional 45- to 55-minute classes, whereas other schools— sometimes within the same district— prefer a block scheduling system consisting of class periods that range from 75 to 110 minutes. For these reasons, it is difficult to outline a detailed lesson plan that would suit all teachers without modification. However, this Program Manager with Daily Lesson Plans offers a sample framework suggesting how to use the textbook *Navegando 1,* along with accompanying ancillaries. Two models are provided: one for a 50-minute class period meeting, and another for a 90-minute block. Adhering to the suggested lesson plans for either model would make it possible to cover all chapters of the textbook in one school year. The 50-minute class period follows a 19-day plan for chapters 1-9 and 7 days for chapter 10; the 90-minute plan follows a 9-day plan for chapters 1-9 and 7 days for chapter 10. The Achievement Tests are scheduled for one day each (after chapters 5 and 10) and are optional, as are many other ancillary materials. However, remember that these are only suggestions.

Navegando 1 is a program that is very flexible and allows teachers to cover material in the textbook and ancillaries according to the degree of thoroughness suggested by student needs, time and personal teaching style or school resources. For example, some activities and the *Cultura viva* sections may be omitted, depending upon the needs and time limitations set by individual circumstances. The reading section titled Tú lees is optional, thus offering you additional flexibility in matching content to the needs, interests and curriculum requirements of your own particular situation. Dialogs, other narrative material and many activities in *Navegando 1* have been recorded and offer you additional choices about how to present or review the chapter content.

It is a good idea to try to vary your presentations by using as many different resources as possible in order to recombine similar material for your students' diverse learning styles. For example, the Audio CD Program and the Teacher's Resource Kit offer listening comprehension practice; the Video Program allows students an opportunity to observe native speakers using Spanish in contexts that require skills your students are learning; the CD-ROM tutorials and games individualize and personalize instruction; overhead transparencies offer visual support of spoken Spanish and can serve to practice rote material as well as to provide situational contexts for conversations; and the textbook, Workbook and Teacher's Resource Kit activities all offer additional writing practice. Many ancillaries are available to supplement the textbook. For example, in the Activities for Proficiency Manual there are general forms in *Capítulo 1* that can be utilized throughout all of the chapters as well as forms listed in *Capítulo 10* that can be used as review. These program components provide an abundance of textbook-related activities to provide teaching formats that will enable you to customize your teaching to the many and varied learning styles and needs of your students.

Since teachers' approaches to the subject of homework vary, and because of the extensive variety offered by the *Navegando 1* support materials, specific homework assignments are not provided. However, suggestions for including activities from the accompanying ancillaries have been offered to give you an idea of the possible variations this teaching program offers.

Regular Class Period (50 minutes)

Capítulo 1, Lecciones A y B

Day 1

Textbook (*Lección A*)	Support Materials
Chapter opener, pp. xxviii-1 *Vocabulario I, ¿Cómo te llamas?*, p. 2 *El alfabeto*, p. 2 Activity 1, p. 3 *¡Extra!*, p. 3 Activities 2-4, p. 3	Transparencies 1-10 TPR Storytelling Manual *Materiales para hispanohablantes nativos* CD: *Vocabulario I, ¿Cómo te llamas?* (Track 1) Transparency 11 CD: *El alfabeto* (Track 2) Workbook Activities 1-3 Grammar and Vocabulary Activities 1-2 CD: *Los nombres* (Track 3) CD: Activity 1 (Track 4) Listening Activity 1 (Track 1)

Notes

Day 2

Textbook (*Lección A*)	Support Materials
Warm-up: Review vocabulary, alphabet and names (*Vocabulario I, ¿Cómo te llamas?*, p. 2; *El alfabeto*, p. 2) *Diálogo I, ¡Hola!*, p. 4 Activities 5-7, p. 4 *Cultura viva*, p. 5 Activity 8, p. 5 *Estructura*, p. 6 Activity 9, p. 6	Quiz Activities 1-2 Grammar and Vocabulary Activity 3 CD: *Diálogo I, ¡Hola!* (Track 5) CD: Activity 7 (Track 6) Workbook Activities 4-5

Notes

Day 3

Textbook *(Lección A)*	Support Materials
Warm-up: Review punctuation (*Estructura,* p. 6) *Estrategia,* p. 6 Activities 10-11, p. 7 *Vocabulario II, ¿De dónde eres?,* p. 8 *Los números del 0 al 20,* p. 8	Quiz Activity 3 CD: *Estrategia* (Track 7) CD: *Vocabulario II, ¿De dónde eres?* (Track 8) Transparency 12 Workbook Activities 6-7 CD: *Los números del 0 al 20* (Track 9) Workbook Activities 8-10

Notes

Day 4

Textbook *(Lección A)*	Support Materials
Warm-up: Review numbers (*Los números del 0 al 20,* p. 8) Activities 12-15, p. 9 *Diálogo II, ¿De dónde eres, Hugo?,* p. 10 Activities 16-17, p. 10	Listening Activities 2-4 (Tracks 2-4) Grammar and Vocabulary Activities 4-8 Quiz Activity 4 CD: Activities 12-13 (Tracks 10-11) CD: *Diálogo II, ¿De dónde eres, Hugo?* (Track 12) CD: Activity 17 (Track 13)

Notes

Day 5 | **Textbook** (*Lección A*) | **Support Materials**

Warm-up: Review dialog (*Diálogo II, ¿De dónde eres, Hugo?*, p. 10)
Activities 18-19, p. 10
Cultura viva, p. 11
Activity 20, p. 11
Estructura, p. 12
Activities 21-24, pp. 12-13

Quiz Activity 5
CD: Activity 18 (Track 14)
Workbook Activities 11-13
Quiz Activity 6

Notes

Day 6 | **Textbook** (*Lección A*) | **Support Materials**

Warm-up: Review definite articles and countries (*Estructura*, p. 12)
Estructura, p. 13
¡Oportunidades!, p. 14
Activities 25-27, pp. 14-15

Quiz Activity 7
Listening Activity 5 (Track 5)
Workbook Activities 14-15
CD: Activity 25 (Track 15)

Notes

Day 7

Textbook *(Lección A)*

Warm-up: Review cognates (*Estructura*, p. 13)

Activity 28, p. 15

Lectura cultural, ¡Visita las diez maravillas del mundo hispanohablante!, p. 16

Activity 29-30, p.16

Support Materials

Listening Activity 6 (Track 6)

CD: *Lectura cultural, ¡Visita las diez maravillas del mundo hispanohablante!* (Track 16)

CD: Activity 29 (Track 17)

Notes

Day 8

Textbook *(Lección A)*

Warm-up: Review *Lectura cultural, ¡Visita las diez maravillas del mundo hispanohablante!*, p. 16

Autoevaluación, p. 17

Palabras y expresiones, p. 17

¡Extra!, p. 17

Support Materials

Workbook Activity 16

Grammar and Vocabulary Activity 9

Communicative Activities (Information Gap Activities/Postcard Activities/*Funciones de Comunicación*)

Notes

Day 9 — Textbook (*Lección B*)

Warm-up: Review *Autoevaluación*, p. 17
Vocabulario I, Saludos y despedidas, p. 18
Activities 1-2, p. 19
¡Extra!, p. 19
Activity 3, p. 19

Support Materials

CD: *Vocabulario I, Saludos y despedidas* (Track 1)
Transparency 13
CD: Activity 1 (Track 2)
Listening Activities 1-2 (Tracks 7-8)
Workbook Activities 1-4
Grammar and Vocabulary Activities 1-2

Notes

Day 10 — Textbook (*Lección B*)

Warm-up: Review vocabulary (*Vocabulario I, Saludos y despedidas*, p. 18)
Diálogo I, Buenos días, p. 20
Activities 4-5, p. 20
¡Extra!, p. 20
Activity 6, p. 20
Cultura viva, p. 21
Activities 7-8, p. 21

Support Materials

Quiz Activity 1
CD: *Diálogo I, Buenos días* (Track 3)
CD: Activity 6 (Track 4)

Notes

Day 11

Textbook *(Lección B)*

Warm-up: Review dialog and greetings
(*Diálogo I, Buenos días*, p. 20; *Cultura viva*, p. 21)
Estructura, p. 22
Activity 9, p. 22
Estrategia, p. 22
Activities 10-12, p. 23

Support Materials

Listening Activity 3 (Track 9)
Workbook Activities 5-6
Grammar and Vocabulary Activity 3

Notes

Day 12

Textbook *(Lección B)*

Warm-up: Review formal and informal
(*Estructura*, p. 22)
Vocabulario II, ¿Qué hora es?, p. 24
Los números del 21 al 100, p. 25
Activities 13-14, p. 25

Support Materials

Quiz Activity 2
CD: *Vocabulario II, ¿Qué hora es?* (Track 5)
CD: *Los números del 21 al 100* (Track 6)
Transparencies 14-15
CD: Activities 13-14 (Tracks 7-8)
Listening Activities 4-5 (Tracks 10-11)
Workbook Activities 7-9
Grammar and Vocabulary Activities 4-6
Quiz Activity 3

Notes

Day 13

Textbook (*Lección B*)	**Support Materials**
Warm-up: Review numbers (*Los números del 21 al 100*, p. 25)	CD: *Diálogo II, ¿Cómo te llamas?* (Track 9)
Diálogo II, ¿Cómo te llamas?, p. 26	CD: Activities 15-17 (Tracks 10-12)
Activities 15-17, p. 26	Workbook Activity 10
Cultura viva, p. 27	Quiz Activity 4
Activities 18-19, p. 27	Workbook Activity 11
Estructura, p. 28	
Activity 20, p. 28	

Notes

Day 14

Textbook (*Lección B*)	**Support Materials**
Warm-up: Review telling time (*Estructura*, p. 28)	Listening Activity 6 (Track 12)
Activities 21-22, p. 29	Workbook Activities 12-13
¡Extra!, p. 29	Grammar and Vocabulary Activity 7
Lectura personal, p. 30	CD: *Lectura personal* (Track 13)
Activities 23-24, p. 30	

Notes

Day 15

Textbook *(Lección B)*   **Support Materials**

Warm-up: Review *Lectura personal*, p. 30   Quiz Activity 5
Autoevaluación, p. 31   Workbook Activity 14
Palabras y expresiones, p. 31   Communicative Activities (Information Gap
                                                 Activities/Postcard Activities/*Funciones de
                                                 Comunicación*)

Notes

Day 16

Textbook *(Lección B)*   **Support Materials**

Warm-up: Review *Autoevaluación*, p. 31   CD: *¡Viento en popa!, Tú lees, El mundo
Estrategia, p. 32   hispanohablante* (Track 14)
Tú lees, El mundo hispanohablante, p. 32
Activities A-B, p. 33

Notes

Day 17 | Textbook (*Lección B*) | Support Materials

Warm-up: Review using cognates (*Estrategia*, p. 32)
Estrategia, p. 34
Tú escribes, Activities A-B, p. 34
Proyectos adicionales, Activities A-C, p. 35
Estrategia, p. 35

Communicative Activities (Situation Cards)
Activities for Proficiency (General Forms, Activities 1-30)
Activities for Proficiency (Activities 31-41)

Notes

Day 18 | Textbook (*Lección B*) | Support Materials

Warm-up: Continue with *Proyectos adicionales* (Activities A-C, p. 35) and review for test on *Capítulo 1*
Repaso, p. 36
Trabalenguas, p. 36
Vocabulario, p. 37
Estrategia, p. 37

CD: *Trabalenguas* Track 15
CD-ROM Software, *Introducción*
Video/DVD Program, Episode 1
Select an activity from *Capítulo 1* to include in the *Navegando 1* Portfolio Assessment. Suggestion: Checklist appropriate items on appendices A-J, as needed.

Notes

Support Materials

Test on *Capítulo 1*

Test Booklet
CD: Test Activities 1-7 (Tracks 1-7)
Select an activity from *Capítulo 1* to include
in the *Navegando 1* Portfolio Assessment.
Suggestion: Checklist appropriate items
on appendices A-J, as needed.

Notes

Capítulo 2, Lecciones A y B

Day 1

Textbook (*Lección A*)	**Support Materials**
Warm-up: Review test on *Capítulo 1* Chapter opener, pp. 38-39 *Vocabulario I, ¿Quién es?*, p. 40 Activities 1-2, p. 41	TPR Storytelling Manual *Materiales para hispanohablantes nativos* CD: *Vocabulario I, ¿Quién es?* (Track 1) Transparency 16 CD: Activity 1 (Track 2) Listening Activities 1-2 (Tracks 13-14) Workbook Activities 1-2

Notes

Day 2

Textbook (*Lección A*)	**Support Materials**
Warm-up: Review vocabulary (*Vocabulario I, ¿Quién es?*, p. 40) *Diálogo I, ¿Cómo se llama ella?*, p. 42 Activities 3-5, p. 42 *Cultura viva*, p. 43 Activities 6-7, p. 43	Quiz Activity 1 CD: *Diálogo I, ¿Cómo se llama ella?* (Track 3) CD: Activities 3-5 (Tracks 4-6) Workbook Activities 3-4

Notes

Day 3

Textbook *(Lección A)*   **Support Materials**

Warm-up: Review dialog and culture
   (*Diálogo I, ¿Cómo se llama ella?*, p. 42;
Cultura viva, p. 43)
Estructura, p. 44
Activities 8-10, p. 45
¡Extra!, p. 45
Activities 11-13, p. 46

CD: Activity 10 (Track 7)
Listening Activity 3 (Track 15)
Workbook Activities 5-8
Grammar and Vocabulary Activities 1-3

Notes

Day 4

Textbook *(Lección A)*   **Support Materials**

Warm-up: Review subject pronouns and *ser*
   (*Estructura*, p. 44)
¡Extra!, p. 47
Activities 14-15, p. 47
Vocabulario II, ¿Qué hay en la clase?,
   pp. 48-49
Activities 16-17, p. 49
*Diálogo II, La nueva estudiante de Los
   Ángeles*, p. 50
Activity 18, p. 50
¡Extra!, p. 50

Quiz Activity 2
CD: *Vocabulario II, ¿Qué hay en la clase?*
   (Track 8)
Transparencies 17-18
CD: Activity 16 (Track 9)
Listening Activities 4-5 (Tracks 16-17)
Workbook Activities 9-11
Grammar and Vocabulary Activity 4
CD: *Diálogo II, La nueva estudiante de Los
   Ángeles* (Track 10)
CD: Activity 18 (Track 11)

Notes

Day 5

Textbook (*Lección A*)

Warmup: Review vocabulary and dialog (*Vocabulario II, ¿Qué hay en la clase?*, pp. 48-49; *Diálogo II, La nueva estudiante de Los Ángeles*, p. 50)
Activities 19-21, p. 50
Cultura viva, p. 51
Activity 22, p. 51
¡Oportunidades!, p. 51

Support Materials

Quiz Activity 3
CD: Activities 19-20 (Tracks 12-13)
Listening Activity 6 (Track 18)

Notes

Day 6

Textbook (*Lección A*)

Warm-up: Review culture (*Cultura viva*, p. 51)
Estructura, p. 52
¡Extra!, p. 52
Activities 23-27, pp. 53-54
¡Extra!, p. 54
Activities 28-29, p. 55

Support Materials

Quiz Activity 4
CD: Activity 23 (Track 14)
Listening Activity 7 (Track 19)
Workbook Activities 12-13
Grammar and Vocabulary Activities 5-7

Notes

Day 7

Textbook *(Lección A)*

Warm-up: Review using definite articles
   with nouns (*Estructura*, p. 52)
Estructura, p. 55
¡Extra!, p. 55
Activities 30-34, pp. 56-57
Lectura cultural, La Ola de gira, p. 58
Activity 35, p. 58

Support Materials

Quiz Activities 5-6
Listening Activity 8 (Track 20)
Workbook Activities 14-16
Grammar and Vocabulary Activity 8
CD: *Lectura cultural, La Ola de gira*
   (Track 15)
CD: Activity 35 (Track 16)

Notes

Day 8

Textbook *(Lección A)*

Warm-up: Review using indefinite articles
   with nouns and culture (*Estructura*, p. 55;
   Lectura cultural, La Ola de gira, p. 58)
Activity 36, p. 58
Autoevaluación, p. 59
Palabras y expresiones, p. 59

Support Materials

Quiz Activity 7
Workbook Activity 17
Communicative Activities (Information Gap
   Activities/Postcard Activities/*Funciones de
   Comunicación*)

Notes

Day 9

Textbook *(Lección B)*

Warm-up: Review *Autoevaluación*, p.59
Vocabulario I, Las clases, pp. 60-61
Activities 1-3, p. 61
¡Extra!, p. 61

Support Materials

CD: *Vocabulario I, Las clases* (Track 1)
Transparency 19
CD: Activity 1 (Track 2)
Listening Activity 1 (Track 21)
Workbook Activities 1-3
Grammar and Vocabulary Activities 1-5

Notes

Day 10

Textbook *(Lección B)*

Warm-up: Review vocabulary (*Vocabulario I, Las clases*, pp. 60-61)
Diálogo I, El horario de clases, p. 62
Activities 4-6, p. 62
¡Extra!, p. 62
Cultura viva, p. 63
¡Extra!, p. 63
Activities 7-8, p. 63

Support Materials

Quiz Activity 1
CD: *Diálogo I, El horario de clases* (Track 3)
CD: Activities 4-6 (Tracks 4-6)
Workbook Activity 4

Notes

Day 11

Textbook *(Lección B)*

Support Materials

Warm-up: Review culture (*Cultura viva*, p. 63)
Repaso rápido, p. 64
Activity 9, p. 64
Estructura, pp. 64-65
Activities 10-12, pp. 65-66

CD: Activities 9-10 (Track 7-8)
Listening Activity 2 (Track 22)
Workbook Activities 5-6
Grammar and Vocabulary Activities 6-8

Notes

Day 12

Textbook *(Lección B)*

Support Materials

Warm-up: Review using adjectives to describe (*Estructura*, pp. 64-65)
Activities 13-14, pp. 66-67
Estructura, p. 67
Estrategia, p. 68
Activities 15-21, pp. 68-70

Quiz Activity 2
Listening Activity 3 (Track 23)
Workbook Activities 7-8
Grammar and Vocabulary Activities 9-10
CD: Activity 16 (Track 9)

Notes

Day 13	**Textbook** *(Lección B)*	**Support Materials**
	Warm-up: Review present tense of *-ar* verbs (*Estructura*, p. 67)	Quiz Activity 3
	Estructura, p. 70	CD: Activity 22 (Track 10)
	Activities 22-25, pp. 70-71	Listening Activity 4 (Track 24)
	Vocabulario II, ¿Dónde está?, pp. 72-73	Workbook Activity 9
	Activities 26-28, p. 73	Grammar and Vocabulary Activity 11
	¡Extra!, p. 73	CD: *Vocabulario II, ¿Dónde está?* (Track 11)
		Transparency 20
		CD: Activity 26 (Track 12)
		Listening Activities 5-6 (Tracks 25-26)
		Workbook Activities 10-11
		Grammar and Vocabulary Activities 12-13

Notes

Day 14	**Textbook** *(Lección B)*	**Support Materials**
	Warm-up: Review talking about schedules: *¿A qué hora?* and vocabulary (*Estructura*, p. 70; *Vocabulario II, ¿Dónde está?*, pp. 72-73)	Quiz Activity 4
	Diálogo II, ¿Cuál es tu dirección de correo electrónico?, p. 74	CD: *Diálogo II, ¿Cuál es tu dirección de correo electrónico?* (Track 13)
	¡Extra!, p. 74	CD: Activities 29-30 (Tracks 14-15)
	Activities 29-31, p. 74	Workbook Activity 12
	Cultura viva, p. 75	
	Activity 32, p. 75	

Notes

Day 15

Textbook *(Lección B)*

Support Materials

Warm-up: Review dialog and culture
  (*Diálogo II, ¿Cuál es tu dirección de correo
  electrónico?*, p. 74; *Cultura viva*, p. 75)
Estructura, p. 76
Activities 33-38, pp. 77-79
Lectura personal, p. 80
Activities 39-40, p. 80

Quiz Activity 5
CD: Activity 35 (Track 16)
Listening Activity 7 (Track 27)
Workbook Activities 13-14
Grammar and Vocabulary Activities 14-15
CD: *Lectura personal* (Track 17)
CD: Activity 39 (Track 18)

Notes

Day 16

Textbook *(Lección B)*

Support Materials

Warm-up: Review talking about location
  and how someone feels: *estar* (*Estructura*,
  p. 76)
Autoevaluación, p. 81
Palabras y expresiones, p. 81
Estrategia, p. 82
Tú lees, Puentes y fronteras, p. 82
Activities A-B, p. 83

Quiz Activity 6
Workbook Activity 15
CD: *¡Viento en popa!, Tú lees, Puentes y
  fronteras* (Track 19)
Communicative Activities (Information Gap
  Activities/Postcard Activities/*Funciones de
  Comunicación*)

Notes

Day 17 — Textbook *(Lección B)* Support Materials

Warm-up: Review *Autoevaluación*, p. 81
Tú escribes, p. 84
Estrategia, p. 84
Proyectos adicionales, Activities A-C, p. 85

Communicative Activities (Situation Cards)
Activities for Proficiency (Activities 42-56)

Notes

Day 18 — Textbook *(Lección B)* Support Materials

Warm-up: Continue with *Proyectos adicionales* (Activities A-C, p. 85) and review for test on *Capítulo 2*
Repaso, p. 86
Trabalenguas, p. 86
Vocabulario, p. 87

CD: *Trabalenguas* (Track 20)
CD-ROM Software, *Introducción*
Video/DVD Program, Episode 2
Select an activity from *Capítulo 2* to include in the *Navegando 1* Portfolio Assessment. Suggestion: Checklist appropriate items on appendices A-J, as needed.

Notes

Test on *Capítulo 2*

Test Booklet
CD: Test Activities 1-6 (Tracks 8-13)
Select an activity from *Capítulo 2* to include
in the *Navegando 1* Portfolio Assessment.
Suggestion: Checklist appropriate items
on appendices A-J, as needed.

Notes

Capítulo 3, Lecciones A y B

Day 1

Textbook (*Lección A*)	**Support Materials**

Warm-up: Review test on *Capítulo 2*
Chapter opener, pp. 88-89
Vocabulario I, ¿Adónde vamos en la ciudad?,
    pp. 90-91
Activities 1-2, p. 91
	TPR Storytelling Manual
	Materiales para hispanohablantes nativos
	CD: *Vocabulario I, ¿Adónde vamos en la*
	    ciudad? (Track 1)
	Transparencies 21-22
	CD: Activity 1 (Track 2)
	Listening Activity 1 (Track 28)
	Workbook Activity 1
	Grammar and Vocabulary Activities 1-2
	Workbook Activity 2

Notes

Day 2

Textbook (*Lección A*)	**Support Materials**

Warm-up: Review vocabulary (*Vocabulario I,*
    ¿Adónde vamos en la ciudad?, pp. 90-91)
Diálogo I, En la Ciudad de México, p. 92
Activities 3-5, p. 92
Cultura viva, p. 93
Activities 6-7, p. 93
	Quiz Activity 1
	CD: *Diálogo I, En la Ciudad de México*
	    (Track 3)
	CD: Activities 3-6 (Tracks 4-7)
	Listening Activity 2 (Track 29)
	Workbook Activity 3

Notes

Day 3

Textbook *(Lección A)*　　　　　　　　　　**Support Materials**

Warm-up: Review dialog and culture
　　(*Diálogo I, En la Ciudad de México*, p. 92;
　　Cultura viva, p. 93)
Estructura, p. 94
¡Extra!, p. 94
Activities 8-12, pp. 94-96
Repaso rápido, p. 96
Activity 13, p. 96

Listening Activity 3 (Track 30)
Workbook Activities 4-6
Grammar and Vocabulary Activities 3-5

Notes

Day 4

Textbook *(Lección A)*　　　　　　　　　　**Support Materials**

Warm-up: Review question-asking words
　　(*Repaso rápido*: question-asking words,
　　p. 96)
Estructura, p. 97
Activities 14-20, pp. 97-99

Quiz Activity 2
CD: Activity 14 (Track 8)
Listening Activity 4 (Track 31)
Workbook Activities 7-9
Grammar and Vocabulary Activities 6-9
Quiz Activity 3

Notes

Day 5

Textbook *(Lección A)*

Warm-up: Review asking questions
  (*Estructura*, p. 97)
Vocabulario II, ¿Cómo vamos?, p. 100
Activities 21-23, p. 101
¡Extra!, p. 101

Support Materials

Quiz Activity 4
CD: *Vocabulario II, ¿Cómo vamos?* (Track 9)
Transparencies 23-24
CD: Activity 21 (Track 10)
Listening Activity 5 (Track 32)
Workbook Activities 10-11

Notes

Day 6

Textbook *(Lección A)*

Warm-up: Review vocabulary
  (*Vocabulario II, ¿Cómo vamos?*, p. 100)
Diálogo II, ¿Qué?, p. 102
Activities 24-26, p. 102
Cultura viva, p. 103
Activity 27, p. 103

Support Materials

Quiz Activity 5
CD: *Diálogo II, ¿Qué?* (Track 11)
CD: Activities 24-26 (Tracks 12-14)

Notes

Day 7 | **Textbook** *(Lección A)* | **Support Materials**

Warm-up: Review dialog and culture
(*Diálogo II, ¿Qué?*, p. 102; *Cultura viva*,
p. 103)
Estructura, p. 104
Activities 28-30, pp. 104-105
¡Extra!, p. 105
Activities 31-34, pp. 106-107

Quiz Activity 6
CD: Activity 31 (Track 15)
Listening Activity 6 (Track 33)
Workbook Activities 12-15
Grammar and Vocabulary Activities 10-12

Notes

Day 8 | **Textbook** *(Lección A)* | **Support Materials**

Warm-up: Review saying where someone is
going: *ir* (*Estructura*, p.104)
*Lectura cultural, El metro de la Ciudad de
México es fantástico*, p. 108
Activities 35-36, p. 108
Autoevaluación, p. 109
Palabras y expresiones, p. 109

Quiz Activity 7
CD: *Lectura cultural: El metro de la Ciudad
de México es fantástico* (Track 16)
CD: Activities 35-36 (Tracks 17-18)
Workbook Activity 16
Communicative Activities (Information Gap
Activities/Postcard Activities/*Funciones de
Comunicación*)

Notes

Day 9

Textbook *(Lección B)*

Warm-up: Review *Autoevaluación*, p. 109
Vocabulario I, En el centro, pp. 110-111
Activities 1-3, p. 111

Support Materials

CD: *Vocabulario I, En el centro* (Track 1)
Transparency 25
CD: Activity 1 (Track 2)
Listening Activity 1 (Track 34)
Workbook Activities 1-2
Grammar and Vocabulary Activities 1-2

Notes

Day 10

Textbook *(Lección B)*

Warm-up: Review vocabulary (*Vocabulario I,
    En el centro*, pp. 110-111)
Diálogo I, Vamos al museo, p. 112
Activities 4-6, p. 112
Cultura viva, p. 113
Activity 7, p. 113
¡Extra!, p. 113

Support Materials

Quiz Activity 1
CD: *Diálogo I, Vamos al museo* (Track 3)
CD: Activities 4-6 (Tracks 4-6)

Notes

Day 11

Textbook *(Lección B)*

Warm-up: Review dialog and culture
  (*Diálogo I, Vamos al museo*, p. 112;
  Cultura viva, p. 113)
Estructura, p. 114
Activities 8-12, pp. 114-115
¡Oportunidades!, p. 115

Support Materials

CD: Activity 8 (Track 7)
Listening Activity 2 (Track 35)
Workbook Activities 3-4
Grammar and Vocabulary Activities 3-5

Notes

Day 12

Textbook *(Lección B)*

Warm-up: Review talking about the future:
  ir a + infinitive (*Estructura*, p. 114)
Vocabulario II, En el restaurante,
  pp. 116-117
Activities 13-15, p. 117
¡Extra!, p. 117

Support Materials

Quiz Activity 2
CD: *Vocabulario II, En el restaurante*
  (Track 8)
Transparency 26
CD: Activity 13 (Track 9)
Listening Activity 3 (Track 36)
Workbook Activities 5-6
Grammar and Vocabulary Activity 6

Notes

Day 13

Textbook *(Lección B)*

Warm-up: Review vocabulary (*Vocabulario II, En el restaurante*, pp. 116-117)
Diálogo II, ¿Qué van a comer?, p. 118
¡Extra!, p. 118
Activities 16-18, p. 118
Cultura viva, p. 119
Activity 19, p. 119

Support Materials

Quiz Activity 3
CD: *Diálogo II, ¿Qué van a comer?* (Track 10)
CD: Activities 16-19 (Tracks 11-14)
Listening Activity 4 (Track 37)

Notes

Day 14

Textbook *(Lección B)*

Warm-up: Review dialog and culture (*Diálogo II, ¿Qué van a comer?*, p. 118; *Cultura viva*, p. 119)
Estructura, p. 120
Activities 20-26, pp. 120-123

Support Materials

Quiz Activity 4
CD: Activity 20 (Track 15)
Listening Activity 5 (Track 38)
CD: Activity 22 (Track 16)
CD: Activity 25 (Track 17)
Workbook Activities 7-11
Grammar and Vocabulary Activities 7-11

Notes

Day 15

Textbook *(Lección B)*

Support Materials

Warm-up: Review present tense of *-er* verbs
    (*Estructura*, p. 120)
Estrategia, p. 123
Activities 27-28, p. 123
Lectura personal, p. 124
Activities 29-30. p. 124

Listening Activity 6 (Track 39)
Quiz Activity 5
CD: *Lectura personal* (Track 18)
CD: Activities 29-30 (Tracks 19-20)

Notes

Day 16

Textbook *(Lección B)*

Support Materials

Warm-up: Review *Lectura personal*, p. 124
Autoevaluación, p. 125
Palabras y expresiones, p. 125
Estrategia, p. 126
Tú lees, Frida Kahlo, una artista universal,
    pp. 126-127
Activities A-B, p. 127

Workbook Activity 12
CD: *¡Viento en popa!, Tú lees, Frida Kahlo,
    una artista universal* (Track 21)
CD: Activities A-B (Tracks 22-23)
Communicative Activities (Information Gap
    Activities/Postcard Activities/*Funciones de
    Comunicación*)

Notes

Program Manager

Day 17 | **Textbook** *(Lección B)* | **Support Materials**

Warm-up: Review *Autoevaluación*, p. 125
Tú escribes, p. 128
Estrategia, p. 128
Proyectos adicionales, Activities A-C, p. 129

Communicative Activities (Situation Cards)
Activities for Proficiency Manual (Activities 57-65)

Notes

Day 18 | **Textbook** *(Lección B)* | **Support Materials**

Warm-up: Continue with *Proyectos adicionales*, p. 129, and review for test on *Capítulo 3*
Activities A-C, p. 129
Repaso, p. 130
Trabalenguas, p. 130
Vocabulario, p. 131

CD: *Trablenguas* (Track 24)
CD-ROM Software, Module 1
Video/DVD Program, Episode 3
Select an activity from *Capítulo 3* to include in the *Navegando 1* Portfolio Assessment. Suggestion: Checklist appropriate items on appendices A-J, as needed.

Notes

Test on *Capítulo 3*

Test Booklet
CD: Listening Comprehension Tests
(Tracks 14-19)
Select an activity from *Capítulo 3* to include
in the *Navegando 1* Portfolio Assessment.
Suggestion: Checklist appropriate items
on appendices A-J, as needed.

Notes

Capítulo 4, Lecciones A y B

Day 1 | **Textbook** *(Lección A)* | **Support Materials**

Warm-up: Review test on *Capítulo 3*
Chapter opener, pp. 132-133
Vocabulario I, Mi familia, pp. 134-135
¡Extra!, p. 135
Activities 1-2, p. 135

TPR Storytelling Manual
Materiales para hispanohablantes nativos
CD: *Vocabulario I, Mi familia* (Track 1)
Transparencies 27-28
CD: Activity 1 (Track 2)
Listening Activities 1-2 (Tracks 1-2)
Workbook Activities 1-2
Grammar and Vocabulary Activities 1-4

Notes

Day 2 | **Textbook** *(Lección A)* | **Support Materials**

Warm-up: Review vocabulary (*Vocabulario I,*
  Mi familia, pp. 134-135)
Diálogo I, En la fiesta del abuelo, p. 136
Activities 3-5, p. 136
Cultura viva, p. 137
Activities 6-7, p. 137

Quiz Activity 1
CD: *Diálogo I, En la fiesta del abuelo*
  (Track 3)
CD: Activities 3-5 (Tracks 4-6)
Listening Activity 3 (Track 3)
Workbook Activity 3

Notes

Day 3

Textbook *(Lección A)*

Warm-up: Review dialog and culture
   (*Diálogo I, En la fiesta del abuelo*, p. 136;
   Cultura viva, p. 137)
Repaso rápido, p. 138
Activity 8, p. 138
¡Extra!, p. 138
Estructura, p. 139
Activities 9-10, p. 140
¡Oportunidades!, p. 140
Activities 11-12, pp. 140-141

Support Materials

Grammar and Vocabulary Activity 5
CD: Activity 9 (Track 7)
Listening Activity 4 (Track 4)
Workbook Activities 4-6
Grammar and Vocabulary Activity 6

Notes

Day 4

Textbook *(Lección A)*

Warm-up: Review expressing possession:
   possessive adjectives (*Estructura*, p. 139)
Estructura, p. 141
Activities 13-18, pp. 142-143
¡Extra!, p. 143

Support Materials

Quiz Activity 2
Listening Activity 5 (Track 5)
CD: Activities 14-15 (Tracks 8-9)
Workbook Activities 7-8
Grammar and Vocabulary Activities 7-8

Notes

Day 5 | **Textbook** *(Lección A)* | **Support Materials**

Warm-up: Review present tense of -*ir* verbs
    (*Estructura*, p. 141)
Vocabulario II, ¿Cómo está?, pp. 144-145
Activities 19-20, p. 145
Diálogo II, ¿Por qué estás triste?, p. 146
Activity 21, p. 146

Quiz Activity 3
CD: *Vocabulario II, ¿Cómo está?* (Track 10)
Transparency 29
CD: Activity 19 (Track 11)
Listening Activity 6 (Track 6)
Workbook Activities 9-10
CD: *Diálogo II, ¿Por qué estás triste?*
    (Track 12)
CD: Activity 21 (Track 13)

Notes

Day 6 | **Textbook** *(Lección A)* | **Support Materials**

Warm-up: Review vocabulary and dialog
    (*Vocabulario II, ¿Cómo está?*, pp. 144-145;
    Diálogo II, ¿Por qué estás triste?, p. 146)
Activities 22-23, p. 146
Cultura viva, p. 147
Activity 24, p. 147
Estructura, p. 148
Activities 25-27, pp. 148-149

Quiz Activity 4
CD: Activities 22-24 (Tracks 14-16)
Listening Activity 7 (Track 7)
Workbook Activities 11-12
Quiz Activity 5

Notes

Day 7

Textbook *(Lección A)*

Warm-up: Review describing people and
   things with *estar* (*Estructura*, p. 148)
Activities 28-31, pp. 150-151
Lectura cultural, ¿Qué es la familia?, p. 152
Activities 32-33, p. 152

Support Materials

Grammar and Vocabulary Activities 9-10
CD: *Lectura cultural, ¿Qué es la familia?*
   (Track 17)
Activities 32-33 (Tracks 18-19)

Notes

Day 8

Textbook *(Lección A)*

Warm-up: Review describing people and
   things with *estar* and culture (*Estructura*,
   p. 148; *Lectura cultural, ¿Qué es la*
   familia?, p. 152)
Autoevaluación, p. 153
Palabras y expresiones, p. 153

Support Materials

Quiz Activity 6
Workbook Activity 13
Communicative Activities (Information Gap
   Activities/Postcard Activities/*Funciones de*
   Comunicación)

Notes

Day 9 | **Textbook** *(Lección B)* | **Support Materials**

Warm-up: Review *Autoevaluación*, p. 153
Vocabulario I, A mí me gusta..., pp. 154-155
Activities 1-2, p. 155
Diálogo I, Me gusta mucho, p. 156
Activity 3, p. 156

CD: *Vocabulario I, A mí me gusta...* (Track 1)
Transparencies 30-31
CD: Activity 1 (Track 2)
Listening Activity 1 (Track 8)
Workbook Activities 1-2
Grammar and Vocabulary Activities 1-2
CD: *Diálogo I, Me gusta mucho* (Track 3)
CD: Activity 3 (Track 4)

Notes

Day 10 | **Textbook** *(Lección B)* | **Support Materials**

Warm-up: Review vocabulary and dialog
   (*Vocabulario I, A mí me gusta...*, pp. 154-
   155; *Diálogo I, Me gusta mucho*, p. 156)
Estrategia, p. 156
Activities 4-5, p. 156
Cultura viva, p. 157
Activity 6, p. 157
Estructura, p. 158
Activities 7-8, pp. 158-159

Quiz Activity 1
CD: Activities 4-5 (Tracks 5-6)
Listening Activity 2 (Track 9)
Workbook Activity 3
CD: Activity 7 (Track 7)
Listening Activity 3 (Track 10)
Workbook Activity 4

Notes

Day 11

Textbook *(Lección B)*

Warm-up: Review dialog and culture
(*Diálogo I, Me gusta mucho*, p. 156;
Cultura viva, p. 157)
Activity 9, p. 159
¡Extra!, p. 159
Estructura, p. 160
Activities 10-17, pp. 160-163

Support Materials

Grammar and Vocabulary Activities 3-6
Quiz Activity 2
Listening Activity 4 (Track 11)
CD: Activities 11-13 (Tracks 8-10)
Workbook Activities 5-6
Grammar and Vocabulary Activities 7-9

Notes

Day 12

Textbook *(Lección B)*

Warm-up: Review using *gustar* to state likes
and dislikes and using *a* to clarify or
emphasize what you are saying
(*Estructura*, p. 158; *Estructura*, p. 160)
Vocabulario II, ¿Cómo son?, pp. 164-165
Activities 18-19, p. 165
Diálogo II, ¿Cómo es ella?, p. 166
Activity 20, p. 166

Support Materials

Quiz Activity 3
CD: *Vocabulario II, ¿Cómo son?* (Track 11)
Transparencies 32-33
CD: Activity 18 (Track 12)
Listening Activity 5 (Track 12)
Workbook Activities 7-8
Grammar and Vocabulary Activities 10-11
CD: *Diálogo II, ¿Cómo es ella?* (Track 13)
CD: Activity 20 (Track 14)

Notes

Textbook (*Lección B*)   **Support Materials**

Warm-up: Review vocabulary and dialog   Quiz Activity 4
  (*Vocabulario II, ¿Cómo son?*, pp. 164-165;   CD: Activities 21-22 (Tracks 15-16)
  Diálogo II, ¿Cómo es ella?, p. 166)   Listening Activity 6 (Track 13)
Activities 20-22, p. 166
Cultura viva, p. 167
Activities 23-24, p. 167

Notes

Textbook (*Lección B*)   **Support Materials**

Warm-up: Review culture (*Cultura viva*,   Quiz Activity 5
  p. 157; *Cultura viva*, p. 167)   CD: Activity 26 (Track 17)
Estructura, p. 168   Listening Activity 7 (Track 14)
Activities 25-30, pp. 168-170   Workbook Activities 9-12
                                               Grammar and Vocabulary Activities 12-13

Notes

Day 15

Textbook *(Lección B)* | **Support Materials**

Warm-up: Review *ser* vs. *estar* (*Estructura*, p. 168)
Activities 31-33, pp. 170-171
Lectura personal, p. 172
Activities 34-35, p. 172

Quiz Activity 6
CD: *Lectura personal* (Track 18)
CD: Activities 34-35 (Tracks 19-20)

Notes

Day 16

Textbook *(Lección B)* | **Support Materials**

Warm-up: Review culture (*Lectura personal*, p. 172)
Autoevaluación, p. 173
Palabras y expresiones, p. 173
Tú lees, El béisbol y la familia Martínez, pp. 174-175
Estrategia, p. 174
Activities A-B, p. 175

Workbook Activity 13
Communicative Activities (Information Gap Activities/Postcard Activities/*Funciones de Comunicación*)
CD: *¡Viento en popa!, Tú lees, El béisbol y la familia Martínez* (Track 21)
CD: Activities A-B (Tracks 22-23)

Notes

Day 17

Textbook *(Lección B)*

Warm-up: Review *Autoevaluación*, p. 173
Tú escribes, Activities A-B, p. 176
Estrategia, p. 176
Proyectos adicionales, Activities A-C, p. 177

Support Materials

Communicative Activities (Situation Cards)
Activities for Proficiency (Activities 66-76)

Notes

Day 18

Textbook *(Lección B)*

Warm-up: Continue working on *Proyectos
   adicionales*, p. 177, and review for test on
   Capítulo 4
Repaso, p. 178
Trabalenguas, p. 178
Vocabulario, p. 179

Support Materials

CD: *Trabalenguas* (Track 24)
CD-ROM Software, Module 1
Video/DVD Program, Episode 4
Select an activity from *Capítulo 4* to include
   in the *Navegando 1* Portfolio Assessment.
   Suggestion: Checklist appropriate items
   on appendices A-J, as needed.

Notes

Support Materials

Test on *Capítulo 4*

Test Booklet
CD: Listening Comprehension Tests
(Tracks 20-25)
Select an activity from *Capítulo 4* to include
in the *Navegando 1* Portfolio Assessment.
Suggestion: Checklist appropriate items
on appendices A-J, as needed.

Notes

Capítulo 5, Lecciones A y B

Day 1 | **Textbook** *(Lección A)* | **Support Materials**

Warm-up: Review test on *Capítulo 4*
Chapter opener, pp. 180-181
Vocabulario I, Un sábado en la tienda de artículos electrónicos, p. 182
Activities 1-2, p. 183

TPR Storytelling Manual
Materiales para hispanohablantes nativos
CD: *Vocabulario I, Un sábado en la tienda de artículos electrónicos* (Track 1)
Transparencies 34-35
CD: Activity 1 (Track 2)
Listening Activity 1 (Tracks 15)
Workbook Activity 1
Grammar and Vocabulary Activity 1

Notes

Day 2 | **Textbook** *(Lección A)* | **Support Materials**

Warm-up: Review vocabulary (*Vocabulario I, Un sábado en la tienda de artículos electrónicos,* p. 182)
Diálogo I, Me gustan las tiendas, p. 184
Activities 3-5, p. 184
Cultura viva, p. 185
Activity 6, p. 185
¡Oportunidades!, p. 185

Quiz Activity 1
CD: *Diálogo I, Me gustan las tiendas* (Track 3)
CD: Activities 3-5 (Tracks 4-6)
Listening Activity 2 (Track 16)
Workbook Activity 2

Notes

Day 3

Textbook *(Lección A)*

Warm-up: Review dialog and culture
(*Diálogo I, Me gustan las tiendas*, p. 184;
Cultura viva, p. 185)
Estructura, p. 186
Activities 7-10, pp. 186-187
¡Extra!, p. 187
Activity 11, p. 188
Estructura, p. 188
Activities 12-14, pp. 188-189

Support Materials

Listening Activity 3 (Track 17)
Workbook Activities 3-5
Grammar and Vocabulary Activities 2-4
CD: Activity 9 (Track 7)
Listening Activity 4 (Track 18)
Workbook Activity 6
Grammar and Vocabulary Activity 5
CD: Activity 14 (Track 8)

Notes

Day 4

Textbook *(Lección A)*

Warm-up: Review saying what someone has:
tener and expressing strong feelings with
¡Qué (+ adjective/noun)*!* (*Estructura*,
p. 186; *Estructura*, p. 188)
Activity 15, p. 189
*Vocabulario II, Las actividades de Virginia la
semana que viene*, p. 190
Activities 16-18, p. 191
¡Extra!, p. 191

Support Materials

Quiz Activities 2-3
CD: *Vocabulario II, Las actividades de
Virginia la semana que viene* (Track 9)
Transparency 36
CD: Activity 16 (Track 10)
Listening Activities 5-6 (Tracks 19-20)
Workbook Activity 7
Grammar and Vocabulary Activities 6-7

Notes

Day 5 | **Textbook** (*Lección A*) | **Support Materials**

Warm-up: Review vocabulary (*Vocabulario II, Las actividades de Virginia la semana que viene*, p. 190)
Diálogo II, ¡Qué semana!, p. 192
Activities 19-22, p. 192
Cultura viva, p. 193
Activity 23, p. 193

Quiz Activity 4
CD: *Diálogo II, ¡Qué semana!* (Track 11)
CD: Activities 19-22 (Tracks 12-15)

Notes

Day 6 | **Textbook** (*Lección A*) | **Support Materials**

Warm-up: Review dialog and culture (*Diálogo II, ¡Qué semana!*, p. 192; *Cultura viva*, p. 193)
Estructura, p. 194
Activities 24-26, pp. 195-196
Estrategia, p. 196
Activities 27-28, p. 196

Quiz Activity 5
CD: Activity 25-26 (Tracks 16-17)
Listening Activity 7 (Track 21)
CD: Activity 28 (Track 18)
Workbook Activities 8-13
Grammar and Vocabulary Activities 8-11

Notes

Day 7

Textbook *(Lección A)*

Warm-up: Review direct object pronouns
  (*Estructura*, p. 194)
Activities 29-31, p. 197
Lectura cultural, Los chicos ticos, p. 198
Activities 32-33, p. 198

Support Materials

CD: *Lectura cultural, Los chicos ticos*
  (Track 19)
Activities 32-33 (Tracks 20-21)
Quiz Activity 6

Notes

Day 8

Textbook *(Lección A)*

Warm-up: Review direct object pronouns
  and culture (*Estructura*, p. 194; *Lectura
  cultural*, 198)
Autoevaluación, p. 199
Palabras y expresiones, p. 199

Support Materials

Quiz Activity 7
Workbook Activity 14
Communicative Activities (Information Gap
  Activities/Postcard Activities/*Funciones de
  Comunicación*)

Notes

Day 9 | Textbook (Lección B)

Warm-up: Review *Autoevaluación*, p. 199
Vocabulario I, La fecha, p. 200
Activity 1, p. 201
¡Extra!, p. 201
Activities 2-3, p. 201

Support Materials

CD: *Vocabulario I, La fecha* (Track 1)
Transparency 37
CD: Activity 1 (Track 2)
Listening Activity 1 (Track 22)
CD: Activity 3 (Track 3)
Workbook Activities 1-2
Grammar and Vocabulary Activities 1-2

Notes

Day 10 | Textbook (Lección B)

Warm-up: Review vocabulary (*Vocabulario I, La fecha*, p. 200)
Diálogo I, ¿Cuándo es tu cumpleaños?, p. 202
Activities 4-6, p. 202
Cultura viva, p. 203
Activities 7-8, p. 203

Support Materials

Quiz Activity 1
CD: *Diálogo I, ¿Cuándo es tu cumpleaños?* (Track 4)
CD: Activities 4-7 (Tracks 5-8)
Listening Activity 2 (Track 23)
Workbook Activity 3

Notes

Day 11

Textbook *(Lección B)*   **Support Materials**

Warm-up: Review dialog and culture
  (*Diálogo I, ¿Cuándo es tu cumpleaños?*,
  p. 202; *Cultura viva*, p. 203)
Estructura, p. 204
Activities 9-10, pp. 204-205
Repaso rápido, p. 205
Activity 11, p. 206

CD: Activity 10 (Track 9)
Listening Activity 3 (Track 24)
Workbook Activities 4-6
Grammar and Vocabulary Activities 3-6
Quiz Activity 2

Notes

Day 12

Textbook *(Lección B)*   **Support Materials**

Warm-up: Review telling where someone is
  coming from: *venir* and using present
  tense to indicate the future (*Estructura*,
  p. 204; *Repaso rápido*, p. 205)
Activities 12-13, p. 207
Vocabulario II, Los meses, pp. 208-209
Los números del 101 al 999.999, p. 209
Activities 14-16, p. 209

CD: *Vocabulario II, Los meses/Los números
  del 101 al 999.999* (Track 10)
Transparencies 38-39
Workbook Activity 7
CD: Activities 14-15 (Tracks 11-12)
Listening Activity 4 (Track 25)
Workbook Activities 8-9
Grammar and Vocabulary Activities 7-9

Notes

Day 13

Textbook (*Lección B*)

Warm-up: Review vocabulary (*Vocabulario II, Los meses*, pp. 208-209)
Diálogo II, ¡Feliz cumpleaños!, p. 210
Activities 17-19, p. 210
Cultura viva, p. 211
Activities 20-21, p. 211

Support Materials

Quiz Activity 3
CD: *Diálogo II, ¡Feliz cumpleaños* (Track 13)
CD: Activities 17-19 (Tracks 14-16)
CD: *Cultura viva, Los días de fiesta* (Track 17)
Listening Activity 5 (Track 26)
Workbook Activity 10

Notes

Day 14

Textbook (*Lección B*)

Warm-up: Review dialog and cultural information (*Diálogo II, ¡Feliz cumpleaños!*, p. 210; *Cultura viva*, p. 211)
Estructura, p. 212
Activities 22-25, pp. 212-214

Support Materials

Quiz Activity 4
CD: Activity 23 (Track 18)
Listening Activity 6 (Track 27)
Workbook Activity 11
Grammar and Vocabulary Activity 10

Notes

Day 15

Textbook *(Lección B)*

Warm-up: Review using numbers 101-
   999,999 (*Estructura*, p. 212)
Estructura, p. 214
Activities 26-28, p. 215
Lectura personal, p. 216
Activities 29-30, p. 216

Support Materials

Quiz Activity 5
Listening Activity 7 (Track 28)
Workbook Activity 12
Grammar and Vocabulary Activities 11-13
CD: *Lectura personal* (Track 19)
CD: Activities 29-30 (Tracks 20-21)

Notes

Day 16

Textbook *(Lección B)*

Warm-up: Review culture (*Lectura personal*,
   p. 216)
Autoevaluación, p. 217
Palabras y expresiones, p. 217
Tú lees, Viaje por Costa Rica, p. 218
Activities A-B, p. 219

Support Materials

Quiz Activity 6
Workbook Activity 13
Communicative Activities (Information Gap
   Activities/Postcard Activities/*Funciones de
   Comunicación*)
CD: *¡Viento en popa!, Tú lees, Viaje por Costa
   Rica* (Track 22)
CD: Activities A-B (Tracks 23-24)

Notes

Day 17 | **Textbook** *(Lección B)* | **Support Materials**

Warm-up: Review *Autoevaluación*, p. 217
Tú escribes, Activities A-B, p. 220
Estrategia, p. 220
Proyectos adicionales, Activities A-C, p. 221

Communicative Activities (Situation Cards)
Activities for Proficiency (Activities 77-81)

Notes

Day 18 | **Textbook** *(Lección B)* | **Support Materials**

Warm-up: Continue working on *Proyectos adicionales*, p. 221, and review for test on *Capítulo 5*
Repaso, p. 222
Trabalenguas, p. 222
Vocabulario, p. 223

CD: *Trabalenguas* (Track 25)
Spanish Reader, *La familia Miranda*
CD-ROM Software, Module 2
Video/DVD Program, Episode 5
Select an activity from *Capítulo 5* to include in the *Navegando 1* Portfolio Assessment. Suggestion: Checklist appropriate items on appendices A-E, as needed.

Notes

Day 19

Test on *Capítulo 5*

Test Booklet
CD: Listening Comprehension Tests (Tracks 26-31)
Select an activity from *Capítulo 5* to include in the *Navegando 1* Portfolio Assessment. Suggestion: Checklist appropriate items on appendices A-F, as needed.

Notes

Day 20

Support Materials

Achievement Test I

Test Booklet
CD: Achievement Test I (Tracks 32-43)
Select an activity from *Capítulo 5* to include in the *Navegando 1* Portfolio Assessment. Suggestion: Checklist appropriate items on appendices A-F, as needed.

Notes

Capítulo 6, Lecciones A y B

Day 1

Textbook *(Lección A)*	**Support Materials**
Warm-up: Review test on *Capítulo 5*	TPR Storytelling Manual
Chapter opener, pp. 224-225	*Materiales para hispanohablantes nativos*
Vocabulario I, ¿Qué tenemos que hacer en la cocina?, pp. 226-227	CD: *Vocabulario I, ¿Qué tenemos que hacer en la cocina?* (Track 1)
Activities 1-2, p. 227	Transparencies 40-41
	CD: Activity 1 (Track 2)
	Listening Activity 1 (Track 1)
	Workbook Activities 1-2
	Grammar and Vocabulary Activity 1

Notes

Day 2

Textbook *(Lección A)*	**Support Materials**
Warm-up: Review vocabulary (*Vocabulario I, ¿Qué tenemos que hacer en la cocina?*, pp. 226-227)	Quiz Activity 1
Diálogo I, ¿Me vas a ayudar?, p. 228	CD: *Diálogo I, ¿Me vas a ayudar?* (Track 3)
Activities 3-5, p. 228	CD: Activities 3-5 (Tracks 4-6)
Cultura viva, p. 229	Listening Activity 2 (Track 2)
Activity 6, p. 229	Workbook Activity 3

Notes

Day 3

Textbook *(Lección A)*

Warm-up: Review dialog and culture
(*Diálogo I, ¿Me vas a ayudar?*, p. 228;
Cultura viva, p. 229)
Estructura, p. 230
Activities 7-9, pp. 230-231
Estructura, p. 231
Activities 10-11, p. 232

Support Materials

CD: Activity 8 (Track 7)
Listening Activity 3 (Track 3)
Workbook Activity 4
Grammar and Vocabulary Activities 2-3
Workbook Activities 5-8
Grammar and Vocabulary Activities 4-9

Notes

Day 4

Textbook *(Lección A)*

Warm-up: Review expressing obligations
with *tener que* and *deber* and stem-
changing verbs: *e → ie* (*Estructura*,
p. 230; *Estructura*, p. 231)
Activities 12-14, pp. 232-233
¡Oportunidades!, p. 233
Vocabulario II, En la mesa, p. 234
Activities 15-18, p. 235

Support Materials

CD: Activity 12 (Track 8)
Listening Activity 4 (Track 4)
Quiz Activities 2-3
CD: *Vocabulario II, En la mesa* (Track 9)
Transparencies 42-43
CD: Activity 15 (Track 10)
Listening Activity 5 (Track 5)
Workbook Activities 9-11
Grammar and Vocabulary Activities 10-12

Notes

Day 5	**Textbook** *(Lección A)*	**Support Materials**
	Warm-up: Review vocabulary (*Vocabulario II, En la mesa*, p. 234)	Quiz Activity 4
	Diálogo II, ¿Te gusta la sopa?, p. 236	CD: *Diálogo II, ¿Te gusta la sopa?* (Track 11)
	Activities 19-21, p. 236	CD: Activities 19-21 (Tracks 12-14)
	Cultura viva, p. 237	CD: *Cultura viva, Las arepas venezolanas* (Track 15)
	Activity 22, p. 237	CD: Activity 22 (Track 16)

Notes

Day 6	**Textbook** *(Lección A)*	**Support Materials**
	Warm-up: Review dialog and culture (*Diálogo II, ¿Te gusta la sopa?*, p. 236; *Cultura viva*, p. 237)	Quiz Activity 5
		CD: Activity 24 (Track 17)
	Estructura, p. 238	Listening Activity 6 (Track 6)
	Activities 23-26, pp. 239-240	Workbook Activities 12-15
		Grammar and Vocabulary Activity 13

Notes

Day 7

Textbook *(Lección A)*

Warm-up: Review using demonstrative
  adjectives (*Estructura*, p. 238)
Activities 27-28, pp. 240-241
¡Extra!, p. 241
Lectura cultural, Una deliciosa tradición,
  p. 242
Activities 29-30, p. 242

Support Materials

Quiz Activity 6
CD: *Lectura cultural, Una deliciosa tradición*
  (Track 18)
Activity 30 (Track 19)

Notes

Day 8

Textbook *(Lección A)*

Warm-up: Review demonstrative adjectives
  and culture (*Estructura*, p. 238; *Lectura
  cultural*, p. 242)
Autoevaluación, p. 243
Palabras y expresiones, p. 243

Support Materials

Workbook Activity 16
Communicative Activities (Information Gap
  Activities/Postcard Activities/*Funciones de
  Comunicación*)

Notes

Day 9 | **Textbook** *(Lección B)* | **Support Materials**

Warm-up: Review *Autoevaluación*, p. 243
Vocabulario I, La casa de Julián, p. 244
¡Extra!, p. 245
Activities 1-4, p. 245

CD: *Vocabulario I, La casa de Julián* (Track 1)
Transparencies 44-45
CD: Activity 1 (Track 2)
CD: Activity 3 (Track 3)
Listening Activity 1 (Track 7)
Workbook Activities 1-3
Grammar and Vocabulary Activities 1-4

Notes

Day 10 | **Textbook** *(Lección B)* | **Support Materials**

Warm-up: Review vocabulary (*Vocabulario I,*
  La casa de Julián, p. 244)
Diálogo I, La casa de Elisa, p. 246
Activities 5-7, p. 246
Cultura viva, p. 247
Activities 8-9, p. 247

Quiz Activity 1
CD: *Diálogo I, La casa de Elisa* (Track 4)
CD: Activities 5-8 (Tracks 5-8)
Listening Activity 2 (Track 8)
Workbook Activity 4

Notes

Day 11

Textbook *(Lección B)*	Support Materials
Warm-up: Review dialog and culture (*Diálogo I, La casa de Elisa*, p. 244; *Cultura viva*, p. 247) *Estructura*, p. 248 Activities 10-12, pp. 248-249	CD: Activity 10 (Track 9) Listening Activities 3-4 (Tracks 9-10) Workbook Activities 5-7 Grammar and Vocabulary Activity 5

Notes

Day 12

Textbook *(Lección B)*	Support Materials
Warm-up: Review telling what someone says: *decir* (*Estructura*, p. 248) *Estructura*, p. 250 Activities 13-17, pp. 250-251 *Estrategia*, p. 251 *Vocabulario II, Un día en casa*, pp. 252-253 Activities 18-19, p. 253	Quiz Activity 2 Grammar and Vocabulary Activity 6 CD: *Vocabulario II, Un día en casa* (Track 10) Transparency 46 CD: Activities 18-19 (Tracks 11-12) Listening Activity 5 (Track 11) Workbook Activities 8-10 Grammar and Vocabulary Activities 7-8

Notes

Day 13

Textbook (*Lección B*)	Support Materials
Warm-up: Review vocabulary and expressing wishes with *querer* and *gustaría* (*Vocabulario II, Un día en casa*, pp. 252-253; *Estructura*, p. 250) *Diálogo II, Tengo mucho calor*, p. 254 Activities 20-22, p. 254 *Cultura viva*, p. 255 Activities 23-24, p. 255	Quiz Activity 3 CD: *Diálogo II, Tengo mucho calor* (Track 13) CD: Activities 20-22 (Tracks 14-16)

Notes

Day 14

Textbook (*Lección B*)	Support Materials
Warm-up: Review dialog and culture (*Diálogo II, Tengo mucho calor*, p. 254; *Cultura viva*, p. 255) *Repaso rápido*, p. 256 Activity 25, p. 256 *Estructura*, p. 257 *¡Extra!*, p. 257 Activities 26-29, pp. 257-258	Quiz Activities 4-5 CD: Activity 29 (Track 17) Listening Activity 6 (Track 12) Workbook Activities 11-12 Grammar and Vocabulary Activities 9-11

Notes

Day 15

Textbook (*Lección B*)

Warm-up: Review regular present-tense
    verbs and stem-changing verbs *e → i*
    (*Repaso rápido*, p. 256; *Estructura*, p. 257)
Activities 30-32, p. 259
Lectura personal, p. 260
Activities 33-34, p. 260

Support Materials

Listening Activity 7 (Track 13)
Workbook Activities 13-14
Quiz Activity 6
Grammar and Vocabulary Activity 12
CD: *Lectura personal* (Track 18)
CD: Activities 33-34 (Tracks 19-20)

Notes

Day 16

Textbook (*Lección B*)

Warm-up: Review culture (*Lectura personal*,
    p. 260)
Autoevaluación, p. 261
Palabras y expresiones, p. 261
Estrategia, p. 262
Tú lees, La casa de mis sueños, pp. 262-263
Activities A-B, p. 263

Support Materials

Workbook Activity 15
Communicative Activities (Information Gap
    Activities/Postcard Activities/*Funciones de
    Comunicación*)
CD: *¡Viento en popa!, Tú lees, La casa de mis
    sueños* (Track 21)
CD: Activities A-B (Tracks 22-23)

Notes

Day 17 | **Textbook** *(Lección B)* | **Support Materials**

Warm-up: Review *Autoevaluación*, p. 261
Tú escribes, p. 264
Estrategia, p. 264
Proyectos adicionales, Activities A-D, p. 265

Communicative Activities (Situation Cards)
Activities for Proficiency (Activities 82-94)

Notes

Day 18 | **Textbook** *(Lección B)* | **Support Materials**

Warm-up: Continue working on *Proyectos adicionales*, p. 265, and review for test on *Capítulo 6*
Repaso, p. 266
Trabalenguas, p. 266
Vocabulario, p. 267

CD: *Trabalenguas* (Track 24)
CD-ROM Software, Module 2
Video/DVD Program, Episode 6
Select an activity from *Capítulo 6* to include in the *Navegando 1* Portfolio Assessment. Suggestion: Checklist appropriate items on appendices A-J, as needed.

Notes

Support Materials

Test on *Capítulo 6*

Test Booklet
CD: Listening Comprehension Tests
(Tracks 1-5)
Select an activity from *Capítulo 6* to include
in the *Navegando 1* Portfolio Assessment.
Suggestion: Checklist appropriate items
on appendices A-J, as needed.

Notes

Capítulo 7, Lecciones A y B

Day 1 | **Textbook** *(Lección A)* | **Support Materials**

Warm-up: Review test on *Capítulo 6*
Chapter opener, pp. 268-269
Vocabulario I, Los pasatiempos, pp. 270-271
Activities 1-2, p. 271

TPR Storytelling Manual
Materiales para hispanohablantes nativos
CD: *Vocabulario I, Los pasatiempos* (Track 1)
Transparencies 47-48
CD: Activity 1 (Track 2)
Listening Activity 1 (Track 14)
Workbook Activities 1-2
Grammar and Vocabulary Activities 1-3

Notes

Day 2 | **Textbook** *(Lección A)* | **Support Materials**

Warm-up: Review vocabulary (*Vocabulario I,
    Los pasatiempos*, pp. 270-271)
Diálogo I, ¿No quieres jugar al ajedrez?, p. 272
Activities 3-5, p. 272
¡Extra!, p. 272
Cultura viva, p. 273
Activity 6, p. 273

Quiz Activity 1
CD: *Diálogo I, ¿ No quieres jugar al ajedrez?*
    (Track 3)
CD: Activities 3-6 (Tracks 4-7)
Listening Activity 2 (Track 15)
Workbook Activity 3

Notes

Day 3

Textbook *(Lección A)*

Warm-up: Review dialog and culture
   (*Diálogo I, ¿No quieres jugar al ajedrez?*,
   p. 272; *Cultura viva*, p. 273)
Estructura, p. 274
Activities 7-10, pp. 274-275

Support Materials

CD: Activity 7 (Track 8)
CD: Activity 9 (Track 9)
Listening Activity 3 (Track 16)
Workbook Activities 4-7
Grammar and Vocabulary Activities 4-6

Notes

Day 4

Textbook *(Lección A)*

Warm-up: Review stem-changing verbs:
   o → ue and *u → ue* (*Estructura*, p. 274)
Activities 11-12, p. 275
Vocabulario II, El tiempo libre, p. 276
Activities 13-14, pp. 277

Support Materials

Quiz Activity 2
CD: *Vocabulario II, El tiempo libre*
   (Track 10)
Transparency 49
CD: Activities 13-14 (Tracks 11-12)
Listening Activity 4 (Track 17)
Workbook Activities 8-9
Grammar and Vocabulary Activities 7-8

Notes

| **Textbook** *(Lección A)* | **Support Materials**

Warm-up: Review vocabulary (*Vocabulario II, El tiempo libre*, p. 276)
Diálogo II, Quiero alquilar una película, p. 278
Activities 15-17, p. 278
Cultura viva, p. 279
Activity 18, p. 279
Estructura, p. 280
Activities 19-20, pp. 280-281

Quiz Activity 3
CD: *Diálogo II, Quiero alquilar una película* (Track 13)
CD: Activities 15-17 (Tracks 14-16)
CD: Activities 19-20 (Tracks 17-18)
Listening Activity 5 (Track 18)
Workbook Activities 10-11
Grammar and Vocabulary Activities 9-10

Notes

| **Textbook** *(Lección A)* | **Support Materials**

Warm-up: Review dialog, culture and expressions with *hace* (*Diálogo II, Quiero alquilar una película*, p. 278; *Cultura viva*, p. 279; *Estructura*, p. 280)
Activity 21, p. 281
¡Extra!, p. 281
Estructura, p. 282
Activities 22-26, pp. 282-284
Estrategia, p. 284
Repaso rápido, p. 284

Quiz Activity 4
CD: Activity 22 (Track 19)
Listening Activities 6-7 (Tracks 19-20)
Workbook Activity 12
Grammar and Vocabulary Activities 11-13

Notes

Day 7 | **Textbook** (*Lección A*) | **Support Materials**

Warm-up: Review saying what is happening: present progressive (*Estructura*, p. 282)
Estructura, p. 285
Activities 27-30, pp. 285-286
¡Extra!, p. 286
Activities 31-33, pp. 286-287

Quiz Activity 5
CD: Activities 27-28 (Tracks 20-21)
Workbook Activity 13
Grammar and Vocabulary Activity 14

Notes

Day 8 | **Textbook** (*Lección A*) | **Support Materials**

Warm-up: Review using the present progressive with direct object pronouns (*Estructura*, p. 285)
Lectura cultural, El juego del pato, p. 288
Activities 34-35, p. 288
Autoevaluación, p. 289
Palabras y expresiones, p. 289

Quiz Activity 6
CD: *Lectura cultural, El juego del pato* (Track 22)
Activities 34-35 (Tracks 23-24)
Workbook Activity 14
Communicative Activities (Information Gap Activities/Postcard Activities/*Funciones de Comunicación*)

Notes

Day 9

Textbook *(Lección B)*

Warm-up: Review *Autoevaluación*, p. 288
Vocabulario I, Las estaciones en Chile,
    pp. 290-291
Activities 1-2, p. 291
¡Extra!, p. 291

Support Materials

CD: *Vocabulario I, Las estaciones en Chile*
   (Track 1)
Transparency 50
CD: Activities 1-2 (Tracks 2-3)
Listening Activity 1 (Track 21)
Workbook Activities 1-3
Grammar and Vocabulary Activities 1-2

Notes

Day 10

Textbook *(Lección B)*

Warm-up: Review vocabulary (*Vocabulario I,*
   Las estaciones en Chile, pp. 290-291)
Diálogo I, ¡Vamos a esquiar!, p. 292
Activities 3-5, p. 292
Cultura viva, p. 293
Activities 6-7, p. 293

Support Materials

Quiz Activity 1
CD: *Diálogo I, ¡Vamos a esquiar!* (Track 4)
CD: Activities 3-6 (Tracks 5-8)
Listening Activity 2 (Track 22)
Workbook Activity 4

Notes

Day 11

Textbook *(Lección B)*

Support Materials

Warm-up: Review dialog and culture
(*Diálogo I, ¡Vamos a esquiar!*, p. 292;
Cultura viva, p. 293)
Estructura, p. 294
Activities 8-10, pp. 294-295
Estructura, p. 296
Activities 11-13, pp. 296-297

Workbook Activities 5-6
Grammar and Vocabulary Activity 3
CD: Activity 11 (Track 9)
Listening Activity 3 (Track 23)
Workbook Activities 7-8
Grammar and Vocabulary Activities 4-5

Notes

Day 12

Textbook *(Lección B)*

Support Materials

Warm-up: Review verbs that require special
accentuation and present tense of *dar* and
poner (*Estructura*, p. 294; *Estructura*,
p. 296)
Activities 14-15, p. 297
Vocabulario II, El tiempo, pp. 298-299
Activities 16-18, p. 299

CD: Activity 14 (Track 10)
Quiz Activities 2-3
CD: *Vocabulario II, El tiempo* (Track 11)
Transparencies 51-52
CD: Activities 16-17 (Tracks 12-13)
Listening Activity 4 (Track 24)
Workbook Activities 9-11
Grammar and Vocabulary Activities 6-9

Notes

Day 13 | **Textbook** *(Lección B)* | **Support Materials**

Warm-up: Review vocabulary (*Vocabulario II, El tiempo*, pp. 298-299)
Diálogo II, ¿Qué temperatura hace?, p. 300
Activities 19-21, p. 300
Cultura viva, p. 301
Activities 22-23, p. 301

Quiz Activity 4
CD: *Diálogo II, ¿Qué temperatura hace?* (Track 14)
CD: Activities 19-21 (Tracks 15-17)
Quiz Activity 5

Notes

Day 14 | **Textbook** *(Lección B)* | **Support Materials**

Warm-up: Review dialog and culture (*Diálogo II, ¿Qué temperatura hace?*, p. 300; *Cultura viva*, p. 301)
Estructura, p. 302
Activities 24-26, pp. 302-303
¡Oportunidades!, p. 303
Estructura, p. 304
Activities 27-29, pp. 304-305

CD: Activity 24 (Track 18)
Listening Activity 5 (Track 25)
Workbook Activity 12
Grammar and Vocabulary Activity 10
CD: Activity 27 (Track 19)
Listening Activity 6 (Track 26)
Workbook Activities 13-14
Grammar and Vocabulary Activities 11-12

Notes

Day 15

Textbook *(Lección B)*

Warm-up: Review the endings *-ador* and
  -ista (*Estructura*, p. 304)
Activities 30-31, pp. 306-307
Lectura personal, p. 308
Activities 32-33, p. 308

Support Materials

Workbook Activity 15
Quiz Activity 6
CD: *Lectura personal* (Track 20)
CD: Activities 32-33 (Tracks 21-22)

Notes

Day 16

Textbook *(Lección B)*

Warm-up: Review culture (*Lectura personal*,
  p. 308)
Autoevaluación, p. 309
Palabras y expresiones, p. 309
Estrategia, p. 310
Tú lees, El mundo de los deportes,
  pp. 310-311
Activities A-B, p. 311

Support Materials

Workbook Activity 16
Communicative Activities (Information Gap
  Activities/Postcard Activities/*Funciones de
  Comunicación*)
CD: *¡Viento en popa!, Tú lees, El mundo de
  los deportes* (Track 23)
CD: Activities A-B (Tracks 24-25)

Notes

Day 17

Textbook (*Lección B*)   **Support Materials**

Warm-up: Review *Autoevaluación*, p. 309   Communicative Activities (Situation Cards)
Tú escribes, p. 312   Activities for Proficiency (Activities 95-102)
Estrategia, p. 312
Proyectos adicionales, Activities A-C, p. 313

Notes

Day 18

Textbook (*Lección B*)   **Support Materials**

Warm-up: Continue working on *Proyectos*   CD: *Trabalenguas* (Track 26)
adicionales, p. 313, and review for test on   CD-ROM Software, Module 3
Capítulo 7   Video/DVD Program, Episode 7
Repaso, p. 314   Select an activity from *Capítulo 7* to include
Trabalenguas, p. 314   in the *Navegando 1* Portfolio Assessment.
Vocabulario, p. 315   Suggestion: Checklist appropriate items
                                                              on appendices A-J, as needed.

Notes

Support Materials

Test on *Capítulo 7*

Test Booklet
CD: Listening Comprehension Tests
(Tracks 6-10)
Select an activity from *Capítulo 7* to include
in the *Navegando 1* Portfolio Assessment.
Suggestion: Checklist appropriate items
on appendices A-J, as needed.

Notes

Capítulo 8, Lecciones A y B

Day 1

Textbook (*Lección A*)	**Support Materials**

Warm-up: Review test on *Capítulo 7*
Chapter opener, pp. 316-317
Vocabulario I, Los quehaceres, pp. 318-319
Activities 1-3, p. 319
Estrategia, p. 319

TPR Storytelling Manual
Materiales para hispanohablantes nativos
CD: *Vocabulario I, Los quehaceres* (Track 1)
Transparencies 53-54
CD: Activities 1-2 (Tracks 2-3)
Listening Activity 1 (Track 27)
Workbook Activity 1
Grammar and Vocabulary Activities 1-2

Notes

Day 2

Textbook (*Lección A*)	**Support Materials**

Warm-up: Review vocabulary (*Vocabulario I, Los quehaceres*, pp. 318-319)
Diálogo I, ¿Me ayudas?, p. 320
Activities 4-6, p. 320
Cultura viva, p. 321
Activity 7, p. 321

Quiz Activity 1
CD: *Diálogo I, ¿Me ayudas?* (Track 4)
CD: Activities 4-6 (Tracks 5-7)
Listening Activity 2 (Track 28)
Workbook Activity 2

Notes

Day 3

Textbook *(Lección A)*

Support Materials

Warm-up: Review dialog and culture
(*Diálogo I, ¿Me ayudas?*, p. 320; *Cultura viva*, p. 321)
Repaso rápido, p. 322
Activity 8, p. 322
¡Extra!, p. 322
Estructura, p. 323
¡Extra!, p. 324
Activities 9-13, pp. 324-325

Quiz Activity 2
CD: Activity 8 (Track 8)
Workbook Activity 3
Grammar and Vocabulary Activity 3
CD: Activities 10-11 (Tracks 9-10)
Listening Activities 3-4 (Tracks 29-30)
Workbook Activities 4-6
Grammar and Vocabulary Activities 4-7

Notes

Day 4

Textbook *(Lección A)*

Support Materials

Warm-up: Review direct object pronouns
and indirect object pronouns (*Repaso rápido*, p. 322; *Estructura*, p. 323)
Activities 14-15, pp. 325-326
Estructura, p. 326
Activities 16-18, pp. 326-327
¡Oportunidades!, p. 327
Vocabulario II, Más quehaceres, pp. 328-329
Activity 19, p. 329

Quiz Activity 3
CD: Activities 16-17 (Tracks 11-12)
Listening Activity 5 (Track 31)
Workbook Activity 7
Grammar and Vocabulary Activity 8
CD: *Vocabulario II, Más quehaceres* (Track 13)
Transparencies 55-56
CD: Activity 19 (Track 14)
Grammar and Vocabulary Activities 9-10

Notes

Day 5 | **Textbook** *(Lección A)* | **Support Materials**

Warm-up: Review vocabulary (*Vocabulario II, Más quehaceres*, pp. 328-329)
Activity 20, p. 329
Diálogo II, Hay mucho por hacer, p. 330
Activities 21-23, p. 330
¡Extra!, p. 330
Cultura viva, p. 331
Activities 24-25, p. 331

Listening Activity 6 (Track 32)
Workbook Activity 8
Quiz Activity 34
CD: *Diálogo II, Hay mucho por hacer* (Track 15)
CD: Activities 21-24 (Tracks 16-19)

Notes

Day 6 | **Textbook** *(Lección A)* | **Support Materials**

Warm-up: Review dialog and culture (*Diálogo II, Hay mucho por hacer*, p. 330; *Cultura viva*, p. 331)
Estructura, p. 332
Activities 26-28, pp. 332-333

Quiz Activity 4
Listening Activity 7 (Track 33)
Workbook Activities 9-10
Grammar and Vocabulary Activities 11-12

Notes

Day 7

Textbook *(Lección A)*

Warm-up: Review present tense of *oír* and *traer* (*Estructura*, p. 332)
Estructura, p. 334
Activities 29-33, pp. 334-335

Support Materials

Quiz Activity 5
CD: Activity 31 (Track 20)
Listening Activity 8 (Track 34)
Workbook Activity 11
Grammar and Vocabulary Activity 13

Notes

Day 8

Textbook *(Lección A)*

Warm-up: Review talking about the past: preterite tense of *-ar* verbs (*Estructura*, p. 334)
Lectura cultural, ¿Quién lo hace?, p. 336
Activities 34-35, p. 336
Autoevaluación, p. 337
Palabras y expresiones, p. 337

Support Materials

Quiz Activity 6
CD: *Lectura cultural, ¿Quién lo hace?* (Track 22)
Activities 34-35 (Tracks 22-23)
Workbook Activity 12
Communicative Activities (Information Gap Activities/Postcard Activities/*Funciones de Comunicación*)

Notes

Day 9

Textbook *(Lección B)*	Support Materials
Warm-up: Review *Autoevaluación*, p. 337 *Vocabulario I, El supermercado*, p. 338 Activities 1-2, p. 339 *¡Extra!*, p. 339	CD: *Vocabulario I, El supermercado* (Track 1) Transparencies 57-58 CD: Activity 1 (Track 2) Listening Activity 1 (Track 35) Workbook Activities 1-2 Grammar and Vocabulary Activities 1-5

Notes

Day 10

Textbook *(Lección B)*	Support Materials
Warm-up: Review vocabulary (*Vocabulario I, El supermercado*, p. 338) *Diálogo I, ¿Qué nos hace falta comprar?*, p. 340 Activities 3-5, p. 340 *Cultura viva*, p. 341 Activities 6-8, p. 341 *¡Extra!*, p. 341	Quiz Activity 1 CD: *Diálogo I, ¿Qué nos hace falta comprar?* (Track 3) CD: Activities 3-6 (Tracks 4-6) CD: *Cultura viva, La paella* (Track 7) CD: Activity 6 (Track 8) Listening Activity 2 (Track 36)

Notes

Day 11   **Textbook** *(Lección B)*   **Support Materials**

Warm-up: Review dialog and culture   CD: Activity 10 (Track 9)
   (*Diálogo I, ¿Qué nos hace falta comprar?*,   CD: Activity 12 (Track 10)
   p. 340; *Cultura viva*, p. 341)   Listening Activities 3-4 (Tracks 37-38)
Estructura, pp. 342-343   Workbook Activities 3-6
Activities 9-13, pp. 343-345   Grammar and Vocabulary Activities 6-10

Notes

Day 12   **Textbook** *(Lección B)*   **Support Materials**

Warm-up: Review making comparisons   CD: Activity 15 (Track 11)
   (*Estructura*, pp. 342-343)   Listening Activity 5 (Track 39)
Activities 14-19, pp. 346-347   Quiz Activity 2
Vocabulario II, El mercado, pp. 348-349   CD: *Vocabulario II, El mercado* (Track 12)
Activity 20, p. 349   Transparencies 59-60
                                              CD: Activity 20 (Track 13)
                                              Listening Activity 6 (Track 40)
                                              Workbook Activity 7
                                              Grammar and Vocabulary Activities 11-13

Notes

Day 13   **Textbook** (*Lección B*)   **Support Materials**

Warm-up: Review vocabulary (*Vocabulario*   CD: Activity 21 (Track 14)
   II, El mercado, pp. 348-349)   Workbook Activity 8
Activities 21-22, p. 349   Quiz Activity 3
Diálogo II, Comprando chorizo, p. 350   CD: *Diálogo II, Comprando chorizo*
Activities 23-25, p. 350   (Track 15)
¡Extra!, p. 350   CD: Activities 23-25 (Tracks 16-18)
Cultura viva, p. 351   Workbook Activity 9
Activity 26, p. 351

Notes

Day 14   **Textbook** (*Lección B*)   **Support Materials**

Warm-up: Review dialog and culture   Quiz Activity 4
   (*Diálogo II, Comprando chorizo*, p. 350;   CD: Activity 27 (Track 19)
   Cultura viva, p. 351)   CD: Activity 29 (Track 20)
Repaso rápido, p. 352   Listening Activity 7 (Track 41)
Activity 27, p. 352   Workbook Activities 10-12
Estructura, p. 352   Grammar and Vocabulary Activities 14-15
Activities 28-31, pp. 352-353

Notes

Day 15

Textbook *(Lección B)*   **Support Materials**

Warm-up: Review preterite tense of regular
   -*ar* verbs and preterite tense of *dar* and
   estar (*Repaso rápido*, p. 352; *Estructura*,
   p. 352)
Activity 32, p. 353
Lectura personal, p. 354
Activities 33-34, p. 354

Quiz Activity 5
CD: *Lectura personal* (Track 21)
CD: Activities 33-34 (Tracks 22-23)

Notes

Day 16

Textbook *(Lección B)*   **Support Materials**

Warm-up: Review culture (*Lectura personal*,
   p. 354)
Autoevaluación, p. 355
Palabras y expresiones, p. 355
Estrategia, p. 356
Tú lees, Ir de tapas y a merendar,
   pp. 356-357
Activities A-B, p. 357

Workbook Activity 13
Communicative Activities (Information Gap
   Activities/Postcard Activities/*Funciones de
   Comunicación*)
CD: *¡Viento en popa!, Tú lees, Ir de tapas y
   merendar* (Track 24)
CD: Activities A-B (Tracks 25-26)

Notes

Day 17 | **Textbook** *(Lección B)* | **Support Materials**

Warm-up: Review *Autoevaluación*, p. 355
Estrategia, p. 358
Tú escribes, Activities A-B, p. 358
Proyectos adicionales, Activities A-C, p. 359

Communicative Activities (Situation Cards)
Activities for Proficiency (Activities 103-114)

Notes

Day 18 | **Textbook** *(Lección B)* | **Support Materials**

Warm-up: Continue working on *Proyectos adicionales*, p. 359, and review for test on *Capítulo 8*
Repaso, p. 360
Trabalenguas, p. 360
Vocabulario, p. 361

CD: *Trabalenguas* (Track 27)
CD-ROM Software, Module 3
Video/DVD Program, Episode 8
Select an activity from *Capítulo 8* to include in the *Navegando 1* Portfolio Assessment. Suggestion: Checklist appropriate items on appendices A-J, as needed.

Notes

Test on *Capítulo 8*

Test Booklet
CD: Listening Comprehension Tests
(Tracks 11-16)
Select an activity from *Capítulo 8* to include
in the *Navegando 1* Portfolio Assessment.
Suggestion: Checklist appropriate items
on appendices A-J, as needed.

Notes

Capítulo 9, Lecciones A y B

Day 1

Textbook (*Lección A*)

Warm-up: Review test on *Capítulo 8*
Chapter opener, pp. 362-363
Vocabulario I, En la tienda por departamentos, pp. 364-365
Activities 1-3, p. 365

Support Materials

TPR Storytelling Manual
Materiales para hispanohablantes nativos
CD: *Vocabulario I, En la tienda por departamentos* (Track 1)
Transparencies 61-62
CD: Activity 1 (Track 2)
Listening Activity 1 (Track 1)
Workbook Activities 1-3
Grammar and Vocabulary Activities 1-4

Notes

Day 2

Textbook (*Lección A*)

Warm-up: Review vocabulary
(*Vocabulario I, En la tienda por departamentos*, pp. 364-365)
Diálogo I, ¿Cuál prefieres?, p. 366
Activities 4-6, p. 366
¡Extra!, p. 366
Cultura viva, p. 367
Activities 7-8, p. 367

Support Materials

Quiz Activity 1
CD: *Diálogo I, ¿Cuál prefieres?* (Track 3)
CD: Activities 4-7 (Tracks 4-7)
Listening Activity 2 (Track 2)
Workbook Activity 4

Notes

Day 3

Textbook *(Lección A)*

Warm-up: Review dialog and culture
  (*Diálogo I, ¿Cuál prefieres?*, p. 366;
  Cultura viva, p. 367)
Estructura, p. 368
Activities 9-12, pp. 368-369
Estrategia, p. 369
¡Oportunidades!, p. 369

Support Materials

Quiz Activity 2
Listening Activity 3 (Track 3)
Workbook Activity 5
Grammar and Vocabulary Activity 5

Notes

Day 4

Textbook *(Lección A)*

Warm-up: Review adjectives as nouns
  (*Estructura*, p. 368)
Activities 13-14, p. 370
Estructura, p. 370
Activities 15-19, pp. 371-373

Support Materials

Quiz Activity 3
CD: Activity 16 (Track 8)
Listening Activity 4 (Track 4)
Workbook Activities 6-8
Grammar and Vocabulary Activities 6-8

Notes

Day 5 | **Textbook** *(Lección A)* | **Support Materials**

Warm-up: Review talking about the past: preterite tense of *-er* and *-ir* verbs (*Estructura*, p. 370)
Vocabulario II, Artículos para todos, pp. 374-375
Activities 20-22, p. 375
Diálogo II, Un vestido de seda, p. 376
Activities 23-25, p. 376
Cultura viva, p. 377
Activity 26, p. 377

Quiz Activity 4
CD: *Vocabulario II, Artículos para todos* (Track 9)
Transparency 63
CD: Activity 20 (Track 10)
Listening Activity 5 (Track 5)
Workbook Activity 9
Grammar and Vocabulary Activity 9
CD: *Diálogo II, Un vestido de seda* (Track 11)
CD: Activities 23-25 (Tracks 12-14)

Notes

Day 6 | **Textbook** *(Lección A)* | **Support Materials**

Warm-up: Review vocabulary, dialog and culture (*Vocabulario II, Artículos para todos*, pp. 374-375; *Diálogo II, Un vestido de seda*, p. 376; *Cultura viva*, p. 377)
Estructura, p. 378
Activities 27-31, pp. 379-380

Quiz Activity 5
CD: Activity 27 (Track 15)
Listening Activity 6 (Track 6)
Workbook Activities 10-11
Grammar and Vocabulary Activities 10-12

Notes

Day 7

Textbook *(Lección A)*

Warm-up: Review preterite tense of *ir* and *ser* (*Estructura*, p. 378)
Estructura, pp. 381-382
Activities 32-36, pp. 382-383

Support Materials

Quiz Activity 6
CD: Activities 33-34 (Tracks 16-17)
Listening Activities 7-8 (Tracks 7-8)
Workbook Activities 12-13
Grammar and Vocabulary Activities 13-14

Notes

Day 8

Textbook *(Lección A)*

Warm-up: Review affirmative and negative words (*Estructura*, pp. 381-382)
Lectura cultural, Las molas: símbolo de la cultura kuna, p. 384
Activities 37-38, p. 384
Autoevaluación, p. 385
Palabras y expresiones, p. 385

Support Materials

Quiz Activity 7
CD: *Lectura cultural, Las molas: símbolo de la cultura kuna* (Track 18)
CD: Activity 37 (Track 19)
Workbook Activity 14
Communicative Activities (Information Gap Activities/Postcard Activities/*Funciones de Comunicación*)

Notes

Day 9	**Textbook** (*Lección B*)	**Support Materials**
	Warm-up: Review *Autoevaluación*, p. 385	CD: *Vocabulario I, Regalos* (Track 1)
	Vocabulario I, Regalos, pp. 386-387	Transparencies 64-65
	Activities 1-3, p. 387	CD: Activity 1 (Track 2)
		Listening Activity 1 (Track 9)
		Workbook Activities 1-3
		Grammar and Vocabulary Activities 1-3

Notes

Day 10	**Textbook** (*Lección B*)	**Support Materials**
	Warm-up: Review vocabulary (*Vocabulario I, Regalos,* pp. 386-387)	Quiz Activity 1
		CD: *Diálogo I, Busco un regalo* (Track 3)
	Diálogo I, Busco un regalo, p. 388	CD: Activities 4-6 (Tracks 4-6)
	Activities 4-6, p. 388	Listening Activity 2 (Track 10)
	¡Extra!, p. 388	Workbook Activity 4
	Cultura viva, p. 389	
	Activity 7, p. 389	

Notes

Day 11

Textbook *(Lección B)*

Warm-up: Review dialog and culture
  (*Diálogo I, Busco un regalo*, p. 388;
  Cultura viva, p. 389)
Estructura, p. 390
Activities 8-10, p. 390
Estructura, p. 391
Activities 11-16, pp. 391-393

Support Materials

CD: Activities 8-9 (Tracks 7-8)
Listening Activity 3 (Track 11)
Workbook Activity 5
Grammar and Vocabulary Activity 4
CD: Activities 12-13 (Tracks 9-10)
Listening Activity 4 (Track 12)
Workbook Activities 6-10
Grammar and Vocabulary Activities 5-8

Notes

Day 12

Textbook *(Lección B)*

Warm-up: Review diminutives and preterite
  tense of *leer, oír, ver, decir, hacer* and *tener*
  (*Estructura*, p. 390; *Estructura*, p. 391)
Activity 17, p. 393
Vocabulario II, En la caja, p. 394
Activities 18-19, p. 395

Support Materials

Quiz Activities 2-3
CD: *Vocabulario II, En la caja* (Track 11)
Transparency 66
CD: Activity 18 (Track 12)
Listening Activities 5-6 (Tracks 13-14)
Workbook Activities 11-12
Grammar and Vocabulary Activities 9-10

Notes

Textbook (*Lección B*)	**Support Materials**
Warm-up: Review vocabulary (*Vocabulario II, En la caja*, p. 394) *Diálogo II, ¿Cómo va a pagar?*, p. 396 Activities 20-22, p. 396 *Cultura viva*, p. 397 Activity 23, p. 397	Quiz Activity 4 CD: *Diálogo II, ¿Cómo va a pagar?* (Track 13) CD: Activities 20-22 (Tracks 14-16) CD: *Cultura viva, De compras en Guayaquil* (Track 17)

Notes

Textbook (*Lección B*)	**Support Materials**
Warm-up: Review dialog and culture (*Diálogo II, ¿Cómo va a pagar?*, p. 396; *Cultura viva*, p. 397) *Repaso rápido*, p. 398 Activity 24, p. 398 *Estructura*, pp. 398-399 Activities 25-30, pp. 399-401	Quiz Activity 5 CD: Activity 26 (Track 18) Listening Activity 7 (Track 15) Workbook Activity 13 Grammar and Vocabulary Activities 11-13

Notes

Day 15

Textbook *(Lección B)*

Warm-up: Review prepositions and using
    prepositions (*Repaso rápido*, p. 398;
    Estructura, pp. 398-399)
Activity 31, p. 401
Lectura personal, p. 402
Activities 32-33, p. 402

Support Materials

Quiz Activity 6
CD: *Lectura personal* (Track 19)
CD: Activity 33 (Track 20)

Notes

Day 16

Textbook *(Lección B)*

Warm-up: Review culture (*Lectura personal*,
    p. 402)
Autoevaluación, p. 403
Palabras y expresiones, p. 403
Estrategia, p. 404
Tú lees, Las rebajas de Danté, p. 404
Activities A-B, p. 405

Support Materials

Workbook Activity 14
Communicative Activities (Information Gap
    Activities/Postcard Activities/*Funciones de
    Comunicación*)
CD: *¡Viento en popa!, Tú lees, Las rebajas de
    Danté* (Track 21)
CD: Activities A-B (Tracks 22-23)

Notes

Day 17 | **Textbook** *(Lección B)* | **Support Materials**

Warm-up: Review *Autoevaluación*, p. 403
Estrategia, p. 406
Tú escribes, p. 406
Proyectos adicionales, Activities A-C, p. 407

Communicative Activities (Situation Cards)
Activities for Proficiency (Activities 115-124)

Notes

Day 18 | **Textbook** *(Lección B)* | **Support Materials**

Warm-up: Continue working on *Proyectos adicionales*, p. 407, and review for test on *Capítulo 9*
Repaso, p. 408
Trabalenguas, p. 408
Vocabulario, p. 409

CD: *Trabalenguas* (Track 24)
CD-ROM Software, Module 4
Video/DVD Program, Episode 9
Select an activity from *Capítulo 9* to include in the *Navegando 1* Portfolio Assessment. Suggestion: Checklist appropriate items on appendices A-J, as needed.

Notes

Support Materials

Test on *Capítulo 9*

Test Booklet
CD: Listening Comprehension Tests
(Tracks 17-21)
Select an activity from *Capítulo 9* to include
in the *Navegando 1* Portfolio Assessment.
Suggestion: Checklist appropriate items
on appendices A-J, as needed.

Notes

Capítulo 10, Lecciones A y B

Day 1

Textbook *(Lección A)*	**Support Materials**
Warm-up: Review test on *Capítulo 9*	TPR Storytelling Manual
Chapter opener, pp. 410-411	*Materiales para hispanohablantes nativos*
Diálogo I, Fue un año divertido, p. 412	CD: *Diálogo I, Fue un año divertido* (Track 1)
Activities 1-3, p. 412	Transparency 67
Cultura viva, p. 413	CD: Activities 1-4 (Tracks 2-5)
Activities 4-5, p. 413	Listening Activities 1-3 (Tracks 16-18)
¡Oportunidades!, p. 413	Workbook Activities 1-4
	Grammar and Vocabulary Activity 1

Notes

Day 2

Textbook *(Lección A)*	**Support Materials**
Warm-up: Review dialog and culture	Quiz Activities 1-2
(*Diálogo I, Fue un año divertido*, p. 412;	Listening Activity 4 (Track 19)
Cultura viva, p. 413)	Workbook Activities 5-9
Estrategia, p. 414	Grammar and Vocabulary Activities 2-6
Activities 6-11, pp. 414-415	

Notes

Day 3

Textbook *(Lecciones A y B)*	Support Materials
Warm-up: Review work on Activities 6-11, pp. 414-415	Quiz Activityies 3-4
Lectura cultural, Machu Picchu, p. 416	CD: *Lectura cultural, Machu Picchu* (Track 6)
Activities 12-13, p. 416	CD: Activities 12-13 (Tracks 7-8)
Autoevaluación, p. 417	Workbook Activity 10
Diálogo I, ¿Adónde van de vacaciones?, p. 418	Quiz Activity 5
Activity 1, p. 418	Communicative Activities (Information Gap Activities/Postcard Activities/*Funciones de Comunicación*)

Notes

Day 4

Textbook *(Lección B)*	Support Materials
Warm-up: Review *Autoevaluación*, p. 417, and dialog (*Diálogo I, ¿Adónde van de vacaciones?*, p. 418)	Quiz Activities 4-5
	CD: *Diálogo I, ¿Adónde van de vacaciones?* (Track 1)
Activities 2-3, p. 418	Transparency 68
¡Extra!, p. 418	CD: Activities 1-4 (Tracks 2-5)
Cultura viva, p. 419	Listening Activities 1-6 (Tracks 20-25)
Activities 4-10, pp. 419-421	Workbook Activities 1-5
¡Oportunidades!, p. 421	Grammar and Vocabulary Activities 1-7

Notes

Day 5   **Textbook** *(Lección B)*   **Support Materials**

Warm-up: Review culture and Activities 5-10
(*Cultura viva*, p. 419) and Activities 5-10;
Activities 5-10, pp. 420-421)
Activity 11, p. 421
Lectura personal, p. 422
Activities 12-13, p. 422
Autoevaluación, p. 423
Estrategia, p. 424
Tú lees, Activities A-B, pp. 424-425

Quiz Activities 1-2
CD: *Lectura personal* (Track 6)
CD: Activities 12-13 (Tracks 7-8)
Workbook Activities 6-8
CD: *¡Viento en popa!, Tú lees, Es sólo una cuestión de actitud* (Track 9)
CD: Activity B (Track 10)
Communicative Activities (Information Gap Activities/Postcard Activities/*Funciones de Comunicación*)

Notes

Day 6   **Textbook** *(Lección B)*   **Support Materials**

Warm-up: Review *Autoevaluación*, p. 423,
and review for test on *Capítulo 10*
Tú escribes, p. 426
Estrategia, p. 426
Proyectos adicionales, Activities A-C, p. 427
Repaso, p. 428
Trabalenguas, p. 428

Quiz Activities 3-5
CD: *Trabalenguas* (Track 11)
Communicative Activities (Situation Cards)
Activities for Proficiency (Activities 125-158)
CD-ROM Software, Module 4
Video/DVD Program, Episode 10
Spanish Reader, *El viaje a Guatemala*
Select an activity from *Capítulo 10* to include in the *Navegando 1* Portfolio Assessment. Suggestion: Checklist appropriate items on appendices A-J, as needed.

Notes

Day 7

Test on *Capítulo 10*

Test Booklet
CD: Listening Comprehension Tests
(Tracks 22-25)
Select an activity from *Capítulo 10* to include
in the *Navegando 1* Portfolio Assessment.
Suggestion: Checklist appropriate items on
appendices A-J, as needed.

Notes

Day 8

Support Materials

Achievement Test II

Test Booklet
CD: Achievement Test II (Tracks 26-35)
Select an activity from *Capítulo 10* to include
in the *Navegando 1* Portfolio Assessment.
Suggestion: Checklist appropriate items on
appendices A-J, as needed.

Notes

Block Schedule (90 minutes)

Capítulo 1, Lecciones A y B

Day 1	Textbook *(Lección A)*	Support Materials
	Chapter opener, pp. xxviii-1	Transparencies 1-10
	Vocabulario I, ¿Cómo te llamas?, p. 2	TPR Storytelling Manual
	El alfabeto, p. 2	*Materiales para hispanohablantes nativos*
	Activity 1, p. 3	CD: *Vocabulario I, ¿Cómo te llamas?* (Track 1)
	¡Extra!, p. 3	Transparency 11
	Activities 2-4, p. 3	CD: *El alfabeto* (Track 2)
	Diálogo I, ¡Hola!, p. 4	CD: *Los nombres* (Track 3)
	Activities 5-7, p. 4	CD: Activity 1 (Track 4)
	Cultura viva, p. 5	Workbook Activities 1-3
	Activity 8, p. 5	Grammar and Vocabulary Activities 1-3
	Estructura, p. 6	Listening Activity 1 (Track 1)
	Estrategia, p. 6	Quiz Activities 1-2
	Activities 9-11, pp. 6-7	CD: *Diálogo I, ¡Hola!* (Track 5)
		CD: Activity 7 (Track 6)
		CD: *Estrategia* (Track 7)
		Workbook Activities 4-5

Notes

Day 2

Textbook (*Lección A*)

Warm-up: Review vocabulary, dialog and punctuation (*Vocabulario I, ¿Cómo te llamas?*, p. 2; *El alfabeto*, p. 2; *Diálogo I, ¡Hola!*, p. 4; *Estructura*, p. 6)
Vocabulario II, ¿De dónde eres?, p. 8
Los números del 0 al 20, p. 8
Activities 12-15, p. 9
Diálogo II, ¿De dónde eres, Hugo?, p. 10
Activities 16-19, p. 10
Cultura viva, p. 11
Activity 20, p. 11

Support Materials

Quiz Activity 3
CD: *Vocabulario II, ¿De dónde eres?* (Track 8)
CD: *Los números del 0 al 20* (Track 9)
Transparency 12
CD: Activities 12-13 (Tracks 10-11)
Workbook Activities 6-10
Listening Activities 2-4 (Tracks 2-4)
Grammar and Vocabulary Activities 4-8
Quiz Activities 4-5
CD: *Diálogo II, ¿De dónde eres, Hugo?* (Track 12)
CD: Activities 17-18 (Tracks 13-14)

Notes

Day 3

Textbook *(Lección A)*	Support Materials

Warm-up: Review numbers, vocabulary and
dialog (*Los números del 0 al 20*, p. 8;
Vocabulario II, ¿De dónde eres?, p. 8;
Diálogo II, ¿De dónde eres, Hugo?, p. 10)
Estructura, p. 12
Activities 21-24, pp. 12-13
Estructura, p. 13
¡Oportunidades!, p. 14
Activities 25-28, pp. 14-15

Workbook Activities 11-13
Quiz Activities 6-7
Listening Activity 5 (Track 5)
Workbook Activities 14-15
CD: Activity 25 (Track 15)
Listening Activity 6 (Track 6)

Notes

Day 4

Textbook *(Lección A)*	**Support Materials**
Warm-up: Review definite articles, countries and cognates (*Estructura*, pp. 12-13)	CD: *Lectura cultural, ¡Visita las diez maravillas del mundo hispanohablante!* (Track 16)
Lectura cultural,¡Visita las diez maravillas del mundo hispanohablante!, p. 16	CD: Activity 29 (Track 17)
Activity 29-30, p.16	Workbook Activity 16
Autoevaluación, p. 17	Grammar and Vocabulary Activity 9
Palabras y expresiones, p. 17	Communicative Activities (Information Gap Activities/Postcard Activities/Funciones de Comunicación)
¡Extra!, p. 17	
Vocabulario I, Saludos y despedidas, p. 18	CD: *Vocabulario I, Saludos y despedidas* (Track 1)
Activities 1-2, p. 19	Transparency 13
¡Extra!, p. 19	CD: Activity 1 (Track 2)
	Listening Activities 1-2 (Tracks 7-8)
	Workbook Activities 1-4
	Grammar and Vocabulary Activities 1-2

Notes

Day 5	**Textbook** *(Lección B)*	**Support Materials**

Warm-up: Review *Autoevaluación*, p. 17, and vocabulary (*Vocabulario I, Saludos y despedidas*, p. 18)
Activity 3, p. 19
Diálogo I, Buenos días, p. 20
Activities 4-5, p. 20
¡Extra!, p. 20
Activity 6, p. 20
Cultural viva, p. 21
Activities 7-8, p. 21
Estructura, p. 22
Activity 9, p. 22
Estrategia, p. 22

Quiz Activity 1
CD: *Diálogo I, Buenos días* (Track 3)
CD: Activity 6 (Track 4)
Workbook Activity 5
Listening Activity 3 (Track 9)

Notes

Day 6   **Textbook** *(Lección B)*   **Support Materials**

Warm-up: Review vocabulary, dialog and   Workbook Activity 6
  formal/informal (*Vocabulario I, Saludos y*   Grammar and Vocabulary Activity 3
  despedidas, p. 18; *Diálogo I, Buenos días*, Quiz Activity 2
  p. 20; *Estructura*, p. 22)   CD: *Vocabulario II, ¿Qué hora es?* (Track 5)
Activities 10-12, p. 23   CD: *Los números del 21 al 100* (Track 6)
Vocabulario II, ¿Qué hora es?, p. 24   Transparencies 14-15
Los números del 21 al 100, p. 25   CD: Activities 13-14 (Tracks 7-8)
Activities 13-14, p. 25   Listening Activities 4-5 (Tracks 10-11)
Diálogo II, ¿Cómo te llamas?, p. 26   Workbook Activities 7-9
Activities 15-17, p. 26   Grammar and Vocabulary Activities 4-6
Cultura viva, p. 27   Quiz Activity 3
Activities 18-19, p. 27   CD: *Diálogo II, ¿Cómo te llamas?* (Track 9)
                                                  CD: Activities 15-17 (Tracks 10-12)
                                                  Workbook Activity 10

Notes

Textbook (*Lección B*)	**Support Materials**
Warm-up: Review vocabulary, numbers 21 to 100 and culture (*Vocabulario II, ¿Qué hora es?*, p. 24; *Los números del 21 al 100*, p. 25; *Cultura viva*, p. 27)	Quiz Activity 4
	Listening Activity 6 (Track 12)
	Workbook Activities 11-13
	Grammar and Vocabulary Activity 7
Estructura, p. 28	Quiz Activity 5
Activities 20-22, pp. 28-29	CD: *Lectura personal* (Track 13)
¡Extra!, p. 29	Workbook Activity 14
Lectura personal, p. 30	Communicative Activities (Information Gap Activities/Postcard Activities/*Funciones de Comunicación*)
Activities 23-24, p. 30	
Autoevaluación, p. 31	
Palabras y expresiones, p. 31	

Notes

Textbook (*Lección B*)	**Support Materials**

Warm-up: Review telling time (*Estructura*, p. 28) and *Autoevaluación*, p. 31, and start review for test on *Capítulo 1*
Estrategia, p. 32
Tú lees, El mundo hispanohablante, p. 32
Activities A-B, p. 33
Estrategia, p. 34
Tú escribes, Activities A-B, p. 34
Proyectos adicionales, Activities A-C, p. 35
Estrategia, p. 35

CD: *¡Viento en popa!, Tú lees, El mundo hispanohablante* (Track 14)
Communciative Activities (Situation Cards)
Activities for Proficiency (General Forms, Activities 1-30)
Activities for Proficiency (Activities 31-41)
CD-ROM Software, *Introducción*
Video/DVD Program, Episode 1
Select an activity from *Capítulo 1* to include in the *Navegando 1* Portfolio Assessment. Suggestion: Checklist appropriate items on appendices A-J, as needed.

Notes

Textbook (*Lección B*)

Support Materials

Warm-up: Continue review for test on *Capítulo 1* and review chosen activities from *Tú escribes*, p. 34, and *Proyectos adicionales*, Activities A-C, p. 35

Repaso, p. 36

Trabalenguas, p. 36

Vocabulario, p. 37

Estrategia, p. 37

Test on *Capítulo 1*

CD: *Trabalenguas* Track 15

Test Booklet *Capítulo 1*

CD: Test Activities 1-7 (Tracks 1-7)

Select an activity from *Capítulo 1* to include in the *Navegando 1* Portfolio Assessment. Suggestion: Checklist appropriate items on appendices A-J, as needed.

Notes

Capítulo 2, Lecciones A y B

Day 1 | **Textbook** *(Lección A)* | **Support Materials**

Warm-up: Review test on *Capítulo 1*
Chapter opener, pp. 38-39
Vocabulario I, ¿Quién es?, p. 40
Activities 1-2, p. 41
Diálogo I, ¿Cómo se llama ella?, p. 42
Activities 3-5, p. 42
Cultura viva, p. 43
Activities 6-7, p. 43

TPR Storytelling Manual
Materiales para hispanohablantes nativos
CD: *Vocabulario I, ¿Quién es?* (Track 1)
Transparency 16
CD: Activity 1 (Track 2)
Listening Activities 1-2 (Tracks 13-14)
Workbook Activities 1-2
CD: *Diálogo I, ¿Cómo se llama ella?* (Track 3)
CD: Activities 3-5 (Tracks 4-6)
Workbook Activities 3-4

Notes

Day 2	**Textbook** (*Lección A*)	**Support Materials**

Warm-up: Review vocabulary and dialog
(*Vocabulario I, ¿Quién es?*, p. 40;
Diálogo I, ¿Cómo se llama ella?, p. 42)
Estructura, p. 44
Activities 8-10, p. 45
¡Extra!, p. 45
Activities 11-15, pp. 46-47
¡Extra!, p. 47
Vocabulario II, ¿Qué hay en la clase?,
pp. 48-49
Activities 16-17, p. 49
*Diálogo II, La nueva estudiante de Los
Ángeles*, p. 50
Activities 19-21, p. 50

Quiz Activity 1
CD: Activity 10 (Track 7)
Listening Activity 3 (Track 15)
Workbook Activities 5-8
Grammar and Vocabulary Activities 1-3
CD: *Vocabulario II, ¿Qué hay en la clase?*
(Track 8)
Transparencies 17-18
CD: Activity 16 (Track 9)
Listening Activities 4-5 (Tracks 16-17)
Workbook Activities 9-11
Grammar and Vocabulary Activity 4
CD: *Diálogo II, La nueva estudiante de Los
Ángeles* (Track 10)
CD: Activities 18-20 (Tracks 11-13)

Notes

Textbook (*Lección A*)	**Support Materials**
Warm-up: Review subject pronouns and the verb *ser*, vocabulary and dialog (*Estructura*, p. 44; *Vocabulario II, ¿Qué hay en la clase?*, pp. 48-49; *Diálogo II, La nueva estudiante de Los Ángeles*, p. 50)	Quiz Activities 2-3
	Listening Activity 6 (Track 18)
	Quiz Activity 4
	CD: Activity 23 (Track 14)
	Listening Activity 7 (Track 19)
Cultura viva, p. 51	Workbook Activities 12-13
Activity 22, p. 51	Grammar and Vocabulary Activities 5-7
¡Oportunidades!, p. 51	Listening Activity 8 (Track 20)
Estructura, p. 52	Workbook Activities 14-16
¡Extra!, p. 52	Grammar and Vocabulary Activity 8
Activities 23-27, pp. 53-54	
¡Extra!, p. 54	
Activities 28-29, p. 55	
Estructura, p. 55	
¡Extra!, p. 55	
Activities 30-34, pp. 56-57	

Notes

Day 4   **Textbook** *(Lecciones A y B)*   **Support Materials**

Warm-up: Review using definite and
     indefinite articles with nouns (*Estructura*,
     p. 52; *Estructura*, p. 55)
Lectura cultural, La Ola de gira, p. 58
Activities 35-36, p. 58
Autoevaluación, p. 59
Palabras y expresiones, p. 59
Vocabulario I, Las clases, pp. 60-61
Activities 1-3, p. 61
¡Extra!, p. 61
Diálogo I, El horario de clases, p. 62
Activity 4, p. 62

Quiz Activities 5-7
CD: *Lectura cultural, La Ola de gira*
     (Track 15)
CD: Activity 35 (Track 16)
Workbook Activity 17
Communicative Activities (Information Gap
     Activities/Postcard Activities/*Funciones de
     Comunicación*)
CD: *Vocabulario I, Las clases* (Track 1)
Transparency 19
CD: Activity 1 (Track 2)
Listening Activity 1 (Track 21)
Workbook Activities 1-3
Grammar and Vocabulary Activities 1-5

Notes

Textbook (*Lección B*)	**Support Materials**
Warm-up: Review *Autoevaluación*, p. 59, vocabulary and dialog (*Vocabulario I, Las clases*, pp. 60-61; *Diálogo I, El horario de clases*, p. 62)	Quiz Activity 1
	CD: *Diálogo I, El horario de clases* (Track 3)
	CD: Activities 4-6 (Tracks 4-6)
Activities 5-6, p. 62	Workbook Activity 4
¡Extra!, p. 62	CD: Activities 9-10 (Tracks 7-8)
Cultura viva, p. 63	Listening Activities 2-3 (Tracks 22-23)
¡Extra!, p. 63	Workbook Activities 5-8
Activities 7-8, p. 63	Grammar and Vocabulary Activities 6-8
Repaso rápido, p. 64	
Activity 9, p. 64	
Estructura, pp. 64-65	
Activities 10-14, pp. 65-67	
Estructura, p. 67	
Estrategia, p. 68	
Activity 15, p. 68	

Notes

Textbook (*Lección B*)	Support Materials
Warm-up: Review culture, using adjectives to describe and present tense of *-ar* verbs (*Cultura viva*, p. 63; *Estructura*, pp. 64-65; *Estructura*, p. 67)	Quiz Activity 2
	Grammar and Vocabulary Activities 9-10
	CD: Activity 16 (Track 9)
	Quiz Activity 3
Activities 16-21, pp. 68-70	CD: Activity 22 (Track 10)
Estructura, p. 70	Listening Activity 4 (Track 24)
Activities 22-25, pp. 70-71	Workbook Activity 9
Vocabulario II, ¿Dónde está?, pp. 72-73	Grammar and Vocabulary Activity 11
Activities 26-28, p. 73	CD: *Vocabulario II, ¿Dónde está?* (Track 11)
¡Extra!, p. 73	Transparency 20
Diálogo II, ¿Cuál es tu dirección de correo electrónico?, p. 74	CD: Activity 26 (Track 12)
	Listening Activities 5-6 (Tracks 25-26)
¡Extra!, p. 74	Workbook Activities 10-11
Activities 29-31, p. 74	Grammar and Vocabulary Activities 12-13
	CD: *Diálogo II, ¿Cuál es tu dirección de correo electrónico?* (Track 13)
	CD: Activities 29-30 (Tracks 14-15)

Notes

Day 7

Textbook *(Lección B)*   **Support Materials**

Warm-up: Review talking about schedules: Quiz Activity 4
  ¿A qué hora?, vocabulary and dialog   Workbook Activity 12
  (*Estructura,* p. 70; *Vocabulario II, ¿Dónde*   Quiz Activity 5
  está?, pp. 72-73; *Diálogo II, ¿Cuál es tu*   CD: Activity 35 (Track 16)
  dirección de correo electrónico?, p. 74)   Listening Activity 7 (Track 27)
Cultura viva, p. 75   Workbook Activities 13-14
Activity 32, p. 75   Grammar and Vocabulary Activities 14-15
Estructura, p. 76   CD: *Lectura personal* (Track 17)
Activities 33-38, pp. 77-79   CD: Activity 39 (Track 18)
Lectura personal, p. 80   Workbook Activity 15
Activities 39-40, p. 80
Autoevaluación, p. 81
Palabras y expresiones, p. 81

Notes

Warm-up: Review talking about location or how someone feels: *estar (Estructura,* p. 76) and *Autoevaluación,* p. 81, and start review for test on *Capítulo 2*

Estrategia, p. 82

Tú lees, Puentes y fronteras, pp. 82-83

Activities A-B, p. 83

Tú escribes, p. 84

Estrategia, p. 84

Proyectos adicionales, Activities A-C, p. 85

Quiz Activity 6

CD: *¡Viento en popa!, Tú lees, Puentes y fronteras* (Track 19)

Communicative Activities (Information Gap Activities/Postcard Activities/*Funciones de Comunicación*)

Communicative Activities (Situation Cards)

Activities for Proficiency (Activities 42-56)

CD-ROM Software, *Introducción*

Video/DVD Program, Episode 2

Select an activity from *Capítulo 2* to include in the *Navegando 1* Portfolio Assessment. Suggestion: Checklist appropriate items on appendices A-J, as needed.

Notes

Day 9

Textbook *(Lección B)*

Warm-up: Continue review for test on
Capítulo 2 and review chosen activities
from *Tú lees,* p. 82, *Tú escribes*, p. 84, and
Proyectos adicionales, Activities A-C, p. 85
Repaso, p. 86
Trabalenguas, p. 86
Vocabulario, p. 87
Test on *Capítulo 2*

Support Materials

CD: *Trabalenguas* (Track 20)
CD: Test Activities 1-6 (Tracks 8-13)
Select an activity from *Capítulo 2* to include
in the *Navegando 1* Portfolio Assessment.
Suggestion: Checklist appropriate items
on appendices A-J, as needed.

Notes

Capítulo 3, Lecciones A y B

Day 1	**Textbook** (*Lección A*)	**Support Materials**
	Warm-up: Review test on *Capítulo 2*	TPR Storytelling Manual
	Chapter opener, pp. 88-89	*Materiales para hispanohablantes nativos*
	Vocabulario I, ¿Adónde vamos en la ciudad?, pp. 90-91	CD: *Vocabulario I, ¿Adónde vamos en la ciudad?* (Track 1)
	Activities 1-2, p. 91	Transparencies 21-22
	Diálogo I, En la Ciudad de México, p. 92	CD: Activity 1 (Track 2)
	Activities 3-5, p. 92	Listening Activity 1 (Track 28)
	Cultura viva, p. 93	Workbook Activities 1-2
	Activities 6-7, p. 93	Grammar and Vocabulary Activities 1-2
		CD: *Diálogo I, En la Ciudad de México* (Track 3)
		CD: Activities 3-6 (Tracks 4-7)
		Listening Activity 2 (Track 29)
		Workbook Activity 3

Notes

Textbook *(Lección A)*   **Support Materials**

Warm-up: Review vocabulary and dialog   Quiz Activity 1
   (Vocabulario I, ¿Adónde vamos en la   Listening Activity 3 (Track 30)
   ciudad?, pp. 90-91; *Diálogo I, En la*   Workbook Activities 4-6
   Ciudad de México, p. 92)   Grammar and Vocabulary Activities 3-5
Estructura, p. 94   Quiz Activity 2
¡Extra!, p. 94   CD: Activity 14 (Track 8)
Activities 8-12, pp. 94-96   Listening Activity 4 (Track 31)
Repaso rápido, p. 96   Workbook Activities 7-9
Activity 13, p. 96   Grammar and Vocabulary Activities 6-9
Estructura, p. 97
Activities 14-20, pp. 97-99

Notes

Day 3	**Textbook** (*Lección A*)	**Support Materials**

Warm-up: Review question-asking words
   and asking questions (*Repaso rápido*,
   p. 96; *Estructura*, p. 97)
Vocabulario II, ¿Cómo vamos?, p. 100
Activities 21-23, p. 101
¡Extra!, p. 101
Diálogo II, ¿Qué?, p. 102
Activities 24-26, p. 102
Cultura viva, p. 103
Activity 27, p. 103
Estructura, p. 104
Activity 28, p. 104

Quiz Activities 3-4
CD: *Vocabulario II, ¿Cómo vamos?* (Track 9)
Transparencies 23-24
CD: Activity 21 (Track 10)
Listening Activity 5 (Track 32)
Workbook Activities 10-11
CD: *Diálogo II, ¿Qué?* (Track 11)
CD: Activities 24-26 (Tracks 12-14)

Notes

Textbook (*Lecciones A y B*)	**Support Materials**
Warm-up: Review vocabulary, dialog and saying where someone is going: *ir* (*Vocabulario II, ¿Cómo vamos?*, p. 100; *Diálogo II, ¿Qué?*, p. 102; *Estructura*, p. 104)	Quiz Activities 5-6
	CD: Activity 31 (Track 15)
	Listening Activity 6 (Track 33)
	Workbook Activities 12-15
	Grammar and Vocabulary Activities 10-12
Activities 29-30, p. 105	Quiz Activity 7
¡Extra!, p. 105	CD: *Lectura cultural, El metro de la Ciudad de México es fantástico* (Track 16)
Activities 31-34, pp. 106-107	CD: Activities 35-36 (Tracks 17-18)
Lectura cultural, El metro de la Ciudad de México es fantástico, p. 108	Workbook Activity 16
Activities 35-36, p. 108	Communicative Activities (Information Gap Activities/Postcard Activities/*Funciones de Comunicación*)
Autoevaluación, p. 109	CD: *Vocabulario I, En el centro* (Track 1)
Palabras y expresiones, p. 109	Transparency 25
Vocabulario I, En el centro, pp. 110-111	CD: Activity 1 (Track 2)
Activities 1-3, p. 111	Listening Activity 1 (Track 34)
	Workbook Activities 1-2
	Grammar and Vocabulary Activities 1-2

Notes

| **Day 5** | **Textbook** *(Lección B)* | **Support Materials** |

Warm-up: Review *Autoevaluación*, p. 109, and vocabulary (*Vocabulario I, En el centro*, pp. 110-111)
Diálogo I, Vamos al museo, p. 112
Activities 4-6, p. 112
Cultura viva, p. 113
Activity 7, p. 113
¡Extra!, p. 113
Estructura, p. 114
Activities 8-12, pp. 114-115
¡Oportunidades!, p. 115

Quiz Activity 1
CD: *Diálogo I, Vamos al museo* (Track 3)
CD: Activities 4-6 (Tracks 4-6)
CD: Activity 8 (Track 7)
Listening Activity 2 (Track 35)
Workbook Activities 3-4
Grammar and Vocabulary Activities 3-5

Notes

Day 6

Textbook (*Lección B*)	**Support Materials**
Warm-up: Review dialog and talking about the future: *ir a* + infinitive (*Diálogo I, Vamos al museo*, p. 112; *Estructura*, p. 114)	Quiz Activity 2 CD: *Vocabulario II, En el restaurante* (Track 8) Transparency 26
Vocabulario II, En el restaurante, pp. 116-117	CD: Activity 13 (Track 9)
Activities 13-15, p. 117	Listening Activity 3 (Track 36)
¡Extra!, p. 117	Workbook Activities 5-6
Diálogo II, ¿Qué van a comer?, p. 118	Grammar and Vocabulary Activity 6
¡Extra!, p. 118	CD: *Diálogo II, ¿Qué van a comer?* (Track 10)
Activities 16-18, p. 118	CD: Activities 16-20 (Tracks 11-15)
Cultura viva, p. 119	Listening Activity 4 (Track 37)
Activity 19, p. 119	CD: Activity 22 (Track 16)
Estructura, p. 120	Quiz Activities 3-4
Activities 20-23, pp. 120-121	

Notes

Warm-up: Review vocabulary, dialog and present tense of *-er* verbs (*Vocabulario II, En el restaurante*, pp. 116-117; *Diálogo II, ¿Qué van a comer?*, p. 118; *Estructura*, p. 120)	Listening Activity 5 (Track 38)
	CD: Activity 25 (Track 17)
	Workbook Activities 7-11
	Grammar and Vocabulary Activities 7-11
Activities 24-26, pp. 122-123	Listening Activity 6 (Track 39)
Estrategia, p. 123	Quiz Activity 5
Activites 27-28, p. 123	CD: *Lectura personal* (Track 18)
Lectura personal, p. 124	CD: Activities 29-30 (Tracks 19-20)
Activities 29-30. p. 124	Workbook Activity 12
Autoevaluación, p. 125	Communicative Activities (Information Gap Activities/Postcard Activities/*Funciones de Comunicación*)
Palabras y expresiones, p. 125	

Notes

Day 8

Textbook *(Lección B)*

Warm-up: Review *Autoevaluación*, p. 125
Tú lees, Frida Kahlo, una artista universal,
  pp. 126-127
Estrategia, p. 126
Activities A-B, p. 127
Tú escribes, p. 128
Estrategia, p. 128
Proyectos adicionales, Activities A-C, p. 129

Support Materials

CD: *¡Viento en popa!, Tú lees, Frida Kahlo,
  una artista universal* (Track 21)
CD: Activities A-B (Tracks 22-23)
Communicative Activities (Situation Cards)
Activities for Proficiency Manual (Activities
  57-65)
CD-ROM Software, Module 1
Video/DVD Program, Episode 3
Select an activity from *Capítulo 3* to include
  in the *Navegando 1* Portfolio Assessment.
  Suggestion: Checklist appropriate items
  on appendices A-J, as needed.

Notes

Textbook *(Lección B)*	**Support Materials**
Warm-up: Continue review for test on *Capítulo 3* and review chosen activities from *Tú lees*, pp. 126-127, *Tú escribes*, p. 128, and *Proyectos adicionales*, p. 129 *Repaso*, p. 130 *Trabalenguas*, p. 130 *Vocabulario*, p. 131 Test on *Capítulo 3*	CD: *Trablenguas* (Track 24) Test Booklet CD: Listening Comprehension Tests (Tracks 14-19) Select an activity from *Capítulo 3* to include in the *Navegando 1* Portfolio Assessment. Suggestion: Checklist appropriate items on appendices A-J, as needed.

Notes

Capítulo 4, Lecciones A y B

Day 1	**Textbook** *(Lección A)*	**Support Materials**

Warm-up: Review test on *Capítulo 3*
Chapter opener, pp. 132-133
Vocabulario I, Mi familia, pp. 134-135
¡Extra!, p. 135
Activities 1-2, p. 135
Diálogo I, En la fiesta del abuelo, p. 136
Activities 3-5, p. 136
Cultura viva, p. 137
Activities 6-7, p. 137

TPR Storytelling Manual
Materiales para hispanohablantes nativos
CD: *Vocabulario I, Mi familia* (Track 1)
Transparencies 27-28
CD: Activity 1 (Track 2)
Listening Activities 1-2 (Tracks 1-2)
Workbook Activities 1-2
Grammar and Vocabulary Activities 1-4
CD: *Diálogo I, En la fiesta del abuelo* (Track 3)
CD: Activities 3-5 (Tracks 4-6)
Listening Activity 3 (Track 3)
Workbook Activity 3

Notes

Textbook *(Lección A)*	Support Materials
Warm-up: Review vocabulary, dialog and culture (*Vocabulario I, Mi familia,* pp. 134-135; *Diálogo I, En la fiesta del abuelo*, p. 136; *Cultura viva*, p. 137)	Quiz Activity 1
	Grammar and Vocabulary Activity 5
	CD: Activity 9 (Track 7)
	Listening Activity 4 (Track 4)
Repaso rápido, p. 138	Workbook Activities 4-6
Activity 8, p. 138	Grammar and Vocabulary Activity 6
¡Extra!, p. 138	Listening Activity 5 (Track 5)
Estructura, p. 139	CD: Activity 14(Track 8)
Activities 9-10, p. 140	Workbook Activities 7-8
¡Oportunidades!, p. 140	Grammar and Vocabulary Activities 7-8
Activities 11-12, pp. 140-141	
Estructura, p. 141	
Activities 13-18, pp. 142-143	
¡Extra!, p. 143	

Notes

Day 3

Textbook *(Lección A)*

Warm-up: Review expressing possession: possessive adjectives and present tense of *-ir* verbs (*Estructura*, p. 139; *Estructura*, p. 141)

Vocabulario II, ¿Cómo está?, pp. 144-145

Activities 19-20, p. 145

Diálogo II, ¿Por qué estás triste?, p. 146

Activities 21-23, p. 146

Cultura viva, p. 147

Activity 24, p. 147

Estructura, p. 148

Activities 25-27, pp. 148-149

Support Materials

Quiz Activities 2-3

CD: *Vocabulario II, ¿Cómo está?* (Track 10)

Transparency 29

CD: Activity 19 (Track 11)

Listening Activity 6 (Track 6)

Workbook Activities 9-10

CD: *Diálogo II, ¿Por qué estás triste?* (Track 12)

CD: Activities 21-24 (Tracks 13-16)

Listening Activity 7 (Track 7)

Workbook Activities 11-12

Grammar and Vocabulary Activities 9-10

Notes

Textbook *(Lecciones A y B)*

Support Materials

Warm-up: Review vocabulary, dialog and
   describing people and things with *estar*
   (*Vocabulario II, ¿Cómo está?*, pp. 144-145;
   Diálogo II, ¿Por qué estás triste?, p. 146;
Estructura, p. 148)
Activities 28-31, pp. 150-151
Lectura cultural, ¿Qué es la familia?, p. 152
Activities 32-33, p. 152
Autoevaluación, p. 153
Palabras y expresiones, p. 153
Vocabulario I, A mí me gusta..., pp. 154-155
Activity 1, p. 155

Quiz Activities 4-6
CD: *Lectura cultural, ¿Qué es la familia?*
   (Track 17)
Activities 32-33 (Tracks 18-19)
Workbook Activity 13
Communicative Activities (Information Gap
   Activities/Postcard Activities/*Funciones de
   Comunicación*)
CD: *Vocabulario I, A mí me gusta...* (Track 1)
Transparencies 30-31
CD: Activity 1 (Track 2)

Notes

Textbook *(Lección B)*	**Support Materials**
Warm-up: Review *Autoevaluación*, p. 153, and vocabulary (*Vocabulario I, A mí me gusta...*, pp. 154-155)	Listening Activity 1 (Track 8)
	Workbook Activities 1-2
	Grammar and Vocabulary Activities 1-2
Activity 2, p. 155	Quiz Activity 1
Diálogo I, Me gusta mucho, p. 156	CD: *Diálogo I, Me gusta mucho* (Track 3)
Activity 3, p. 156	CD: Activities 3-5 (Tracks 4-6)
Estrategia, p. 156	Listening Activity 2 (Track 9)
Activities 4-5, p. 156	Workbook Activity 3
Cultura viva, p. 157	CD: Activity 7 (Track 7)
Activity 6, p. 157	Listening Activity 3 (Track 10)
Estructura, p. 158	Workbook Activity 4
Activities 7-9, pp. 158-159	
¡Extra!, p. 159	

Notes

Textbook *(Lección B)*	Support Materials
Warm-up: Review dialog, culture and using *gustar* to state likes and dislikes (*Diálogo I, Me gusta mucho*, p. 156; *Cultura viva*, p. 157; *Estructura*, p. 158)	Grammar and Vocabulary Activities 3-6
	Quiz Activity 2
	Listening Activity 4 (Track 11)
	CD: Activities 11-13 (Tracks 8-10)
Estructura, p. 160	Workbook Activities 5-6
Activities 10-17, pp. 160-163	Grammar and Vocabulary Activities 7-9
Vocabulario II, ¿Cómo son?, pp. 164-165	CD: *Vocabulario II, ¿Cómo son?* (Track 11)
Activities 18-19, p. 165	Transparencies 32-33
Diálogo II, ¿Cómo es ella?, p. 166	CD: Activity 18 (Track 12)
Activities 20-22, p. 166	Listening Activity 5 (Track 12)
Cultura viva, p. 167	Workbook Activities 7-8
Activities 23-24, p. 167	Grammar and Vocabulary Activities 10-11
	CD: *Diálogo II, ¿Cómo es ella?* (Track 13)
	CD: Activities 20-22 (Tracks 14-16)
	Listening Activity 6 (Track 13)

Notes

Textbook *(Lección B)*	**Support Materials**
Warm-up: Review using *a* to clarify or emphasize what you are saying, vocabulary, dialog and culture (*Estructura*, p. 160; *Vocabulario II, ¿Cómo son?*, pp. 164-165; *Diálogo II, ¿Cómo es ella?*, p. 166; *Cultura viva*, p. 167)	Quiz Activities 3-5
	CD: Activity 26 (Track 17)
	Listening Activity 7 (Track 14)
	Workbook Activities 9-12
	Grammar and Vocabulary Activities 12-13
Estructura, p. 168	CD: *Lectura personal* (Track 18)
Activities 25-33, pp. 168-171	CD: Activities 34-35 (Tracks 19-20)
Lectura personal, p. 172	Workbook Activity 13
Activities 34-35, p. 172	Communicative Activities (Information Gap
Autoevaluación, p. 173	Activities/Postcard Activities/*Funciones de*
Palabras y expresiones, p. 173	*Comunicación*)

Notes

Textbook (*Lección B*)	**Support Materials**
Warm-up: Review *ser* vs. *estar* (*Estructura*, p. 168) and *Autoevaluación*, p. 173, and start review for test on *Capítulo 4*	Quiz Activity 6
	CD: *¡Viento en popa!, Tú lees, El béisbol y la familia Martínez* (Track 21)
Tú lees, El béisbol y la familia Martínez, pp. 174-175	CD: Activities A-B (Tracks 22-23)
Estrategia, p. 174	Communicative Activities (Situation Cards)
Activities A-B, p. 175	Activities for Proficiency (Activities 66-76)
Tú escribes, Activities A-B, p. 176	CD-ROM Software, Module 1
Estrategia, p. 176	Video/DVD Program, Episode 4
Proyectos adicionales, Activities A-C, p. 177	Select an activity from *Capítulo 4* to include in the *Navegando 1* Portfolio Assessment. Suggestion: Checklist appropriate items on appendices A-J, as needed.

Notes

Warm-up: Continue review for test on *Capítulo 4* and review chosen activities from *Tú lees*, pp. 174-175, *Tú escribes*, p. 176, *Proyectos adicionales*, p. 177

Repaso, p. 178

Trabalenguas, p. 178

Vocabulario, p. 179

Test on *Capítulo 4*

CD: *Trabalenguas* (Track 24)

Test Booklet

CD: Listening Comprehension Tests (Tracks 20-25)

Select an activity from *Capítulo 4* to include in the *Navegando 1* Portfolio Assessment. Suggestion: Checklist appropriate items on appendices A-J, as needed.

Notes

Capítulo 5, Lecciones A y B

Day 1	**Textbook** (*Lección A*)	**Support Materials**
	Warm-up: Review test on *Capítulo 4*	TPR Storytelling Manual
	Chapter opener, pp. 180-181	*Materiales para hispanohablantes nativos*
	Vocabulario I, Un sábado en la tienda de artículos electrónicos, p. 182	CD: *Vocabulario I, Un sábado en la tienda de artículos electrónicos* (Track 1)
	Activities 1-2, p. 183	Transparencies 34-35
	Diálogo I, Me gustan las tiendas, p. 184	CD: Activity 1 (Track 2)
	Activities 3-5, p. 184	Listening Activity 1 (Tracks 15)
	Cultura viva, p. 185	Workbook Activity 1
	Activity 6, p. 185	Grammar and Vocabulary Activity 1
	¡Oportunidades!, p. 185	CD: *Diálogo I, Me gustan las tiendas* (Track 3)
	Estructura, p. 186	CD: Activities 3-5 (Tracks 4-6)
	Activity 7, p. 186	Listening Activity 2 (Track 16)
		Workbook Activity 2
		Listening Activity 3 (Track 17)

Notes

Textbook *(Lección A)*	**Support Materials**
Warm-up: Review vocabulary, dialog and saying what someone has: *tener* (*Vocabulario I, Un sábado en la tienda de artículos electrónicos*, p. 182; *Diálogo I, Me gustan las tiendas*, p. 184; *Estructura*, p. 186)	Workbook Activities 3-5 Grammar and Vocabulary Activities 2-4 CD: Activity 9 (Track 7) Quiz Activities 1-2 Listening Activity 4 (Track 18)
Activities 8-10, p. 187	Workbook Activity 6
¡Extra!, p. 187	Grammar and Vocabulary Activity 5
Activity 11, p. 188	CD: Activity 14 (Track 8)
Estructura, p. 188	CD: *Vocabulario II, Las actividades de*
Activities 12-15, pp. 188-189	*Virginia la semana que viene* (Track 9)
Vocabulario II, Las actividades de Virginia la semana que viene, p. 190	Transparency 36 CD: Activity 16 (Track 10)
Activities 16-18, p. 191	Listening Activities 5-6 (Tracks 19-20) Workbook Activity 7
¡Extra!, p. 191	Grammar and Vocabulary Activities 6-7
Diálogo II, ¡Qué semana!, p. 192	CD: *Diálogo II, ¡Qué semana!* (Track 11)
Activities 19-20, p. 192	CD: Activities 19-20 (Tracks 12-13)

Notes

Day 3

Textbook *(Lección A)*	Support Materials

Warm-up: Review expressing strong feelings with *¡Qué* (+ adjective/noun)*!*, vocabulary and dialog (*Estructura*, p. 188; *Vocabulario II, Las actividades de Virginia la semana que viene*, p. 190; *Diálogo II, ¡Qué semana!*, p. 192)

Activities 21-22, p. 192
Cultura viva, p. 193
Activity 23, p. 193
Estructura, p. 194
Activities 24-26, pp. 195-196
Estrategia, p. 196
Activities 27-31, pp. 196-197

CD: Activities 21-22 (Tracks 14-15)
Quiz Activities 3-4
CD: Activity 25-26 (Tracks 16-17)
Listening Activity 7 (Track 21)
CD: Activity 28 (Track 18)
Workbook Activities 8-13
Grammar and Vocabulary Activities 8-11

Notes

Day 4

Textbook *(Lecciones A y B)*	Support Materials
Warm-up: Review culture and direct object pronouns (*Cultura viva*, p. 193; *Estructura*, p. 194)	Quiz Activities 5-7
Lectura cultural, Los chicos ticos, p. 198	CD: *Lectura cultural, Los chicos ticos* (Track 19)
Activities 32-33, p. 198	Activities 32-33 (Tracks 20-21)
Autoevaluación, p. 199	Workbook Activity 14
Palabras y expresiones, p. 199	Communicative Activities (Information Gap Activities/Postcard Activities/*Funciones de Comunicación*)
Vocabulario I, La fecha, p. 200	CD: *Vocabulario I, La fecha* (Track 1)
Activity 1, p. 201	Transparency 37
¡Extra!, p. 201	CD: Activity 1 (Track 2)
	Listening Activity 1 (Track 22)

Notes

Day 5 — Textbook (Lección B)

Textbook (*Lección B*)	Support Materials
Warm-up: Review *Autoevaluación*, p. 199, and vocabulary (*Vocabulario I, La fecha,* p. 200)	CD: Activity 3 (Track 3)
Activities 2-3, p. 201	Workbook Activities 1-2
Diálogo I, ¿Cuándo es tu cumpleaños?, p. 202	Grammar and Vocabulary Activities 1-2
Activities 4-6, p. 202	Quiz Activity 1
Cultura viva, p. 203	CD: *Diálogo I, ¿Cuándo es tu cumpleaños?* (Track 4)
Activities 7-8, p. 203	CD: Activities 4-7 (Tracks 5-8)
Estructura, p. 204	Listening Activity 2 (Track 23)
Activities 9-10, pp. 204-205	Workbook Activity 3
	CD: Activity 10 (Track 9)
	Listening Activity 3 (Track 24)
	Workbook Activities 4-6
	Grammar and Vocabulary Activities 3-6

Notes

Textbook (*Lección B*)   **Support Materials**

Warm-up: Review dialog, culture and telling where someone is coming from: *venir* (*Diálogo I, ¿Cuándo es tu cumpleaños?*, p. 202; *Cultura viva*, p. 203; *Estructura*, p. 204)

Repaso rápido, p. 205

Activities 11-13, pp. 206-207

Vocabulario II, Los meses, pp. 208-209

Los números del 101 al 999.999, p. 209

Activities 14-16, p. 209

Diálogo II, ¡Feliz cumpleaños!, p. 210

Activities 17-19, p. 210

Cultura viva, p. 211

Activities 20-21, p. 211

Estructura, p. 212

Activities 22-23, pp. 212-213

Quiz Activity 2

CD: *Vocabulario II, Los meses/Los números del 101 al 999.999* (Track 10)

Transparencies 38-39

CD: Activities 14-15 (Tracks 11-12)

Listening Activity 4 (Track 25)

Workbook Activities 7-9

Grammar and Vocabulary Activities 7-9

CD: *Diálogo II, ¡Feliz cumpleaños!* (Track 13)

CD: Activities 17-19 (Tracks 14-16)

CD: *Cultura viva, Los días de fiesta* (Track 17)

Listening Activity 5 (Track 26)

Workbook Activity 10

CD: Activity 23 (Track 18)

Notes

Textbook *(Lección B)*	**Support Materials**
Warm-up: Review vocabulary, numbers 101 to 999,999, dialog and culture (*Vocabulario II, Los meses*, pp. 208-209; *Los números del 101 al 999.999*, p. 209 and *Estructura*, p. 212; *Diálogo II, ¡Feliz cumpleaños!*, p. 210; *Cultura viva*, p. 211) Activities 24-25, pp. 213-214 *Estructura*, p. 214 Activities 26-28, p. 215 *Lectura personal*, p. 216 Activities 29-30, p. 216 *Autoevaluación*, p. 217 *Palabras y expresiones*, p. 217	Listening Activity 6 (Track 27) Workbook Activity 11 Grammar and Vocabulary Activity 10 Quiz Activities 3-5 Listening Activity 7 (Track 28) Workbook Activity 12 Grammar and Vocabulary Activities 11-13 CD: *Lectura personal* (Track 19) CD: Activities 29-30 (Tracks 20-21) Workbook Activity 13 Communicative Activities (Information Gap Activities/Postcard Activities/*Funciones de Comunicación*)

Notes

Textbook (*Lección B*)	**Support Materials**
Warm-up: Review asking for and giving the date (*Estructura,* p. 214), *Autoevaluación,* p. 217, and start review for test on *Capítulo 5* *Tú lees, Viaje por Costa Rica,* p. 218 Activities A-B, p. 219 *Tú escribes,* Activities A-B, p. 220 *Estrategia,* p. 220 *Proyectos adicionales,* p. 221 Activities A-C, p. 221	Quiz Activity 6 CD: *¡Viento en popa!, Tú lees, Viaje por Costa Rica* (Track 22) CD: Activities A-B (Tracks 23-24) Communicative Activities (Situation Cards) Activities for Proficiency (Activities 77-81) Spanish Reader, *La familia Miranda* CD-ROM Software, Module 2 Video/DVD Program, Episode 5 Select an activity from *Capítulo 5* to include in the *Navegando 1* Portfolio Assessment. Suggestion: Checklist appropriate items on appendices A-E, as needed.

Notes

Textbook *(Lección B)*

Support Materials

Warm-up: Continue review for test on *Capítulo 5* and review chosen activities from *Tú lees*, p. 218, *Tú escribes*, p. 220, and *Proyectos adicionales*, p. 221

Repaso, p. 222

Trabalenguas, p. 222

Vocabulario, p. 223

Test on *Capítulo 5*

CD: *Trabalenguas* (Track 25)

Test Booklet

CD: Listening Comprehension Tests (Tracks 26-31)

Select an activity from *Capítulo 5* to include in the *Navegando 1* Portfolio Assessment. Suggestion: Checklist appropriate items on appendices A-J, as needed.

Notes

Support Materials

Achievement Test I

Test Booklet
CD: Achievement Test I (Tracks 32-43)
Select an activity from *Capítulo 5* to include in the *Navegando 1* Portfolio Assessment. Suggestion: Checklist appropriate items on appendices A-J, as needed.

Notes

Capítulo 6, Lecciones A y B

Day 1	**Textbook** *(Lección A)*	**Support Materials**

Textbook *(Lección A)*

Warm-up: Review test on *Capítulo 5*
Chapter opener, pp. 224-225
Vocabulario I, ¿Qué tenemos que hacer en la cocina?, pp. 226-227
Activities 1-2, p. 227
Diálogo I, ¿Me vas a ayudar?, p. 228
Activities 3-5, p. 228
Cultura viva, p. 229
Activity 6, p. 229

Support Materials

TPR Storytelling Manual
Materiales para hispanohablantes nativos
CD: *Vocabulario I, ¿Qué tenemos que hacer en la cocina?* (Track 1)
Transparencies 40-41
CD: Activity 1 (Track 2)
Listening Activity 1 (Track 1)
Workbook Activities 1-2
Grammar and Vocabulary Activity 1
CD: *Diálogo I, ¿Me vas a ayudar?* (Track 3)
CD: Activities 3-5 (Tracks 4-6)
Listening Activity 2 (Track 2)
Workbook Activity 3

Notes

Textbook *(Lección A)*	**Support Materials**
Warm-up: Review vocabulary, dialog and culture (*Vocabulario I, ¿Qué tenemos que hacer en la cocina?*, pp. 226-227; *Diálogo I, ¿Me vas a ayudar?*, p. 228; *Cultura viva*, p. 229)	Quiz Activity 1
	CD: Activity 8 (Track 7)
	CD: Activity 12 (Track 8)
	Listening Activities 3-4 (Tracks 3-4)
	Workbook Activities 4-8
Estructura, p. 230	Grammar and Vocabulary Activities 2-9
Activities 7-9, pp. 230-231	CD: *Vocabulario II, En la mesa* (Track 9)
Estructura, p. 231	Transparencies 42-43
Activities 10-14, pp. 232-233	CD: Activity 15 (Track 10)
¡Oportunidades!, p. 233	Listening Activity 5 (Track 5)
Vocabulario II, En la mesa, p. 234	Workbook Activities 9-11
Activities 15-18, p. 235	Grammar and Vocabulary Activities 10-12

Notes

Day 3

Textbook *(Lección A)*	Support Materials
Warm-up: Review expressing obligations with *tener que* and *deber* and stem-changing verbs: *e → ie* and vocabulary (*Estructura*, p. 230; *Estructura*, p. 231; *Vocabulario II, En la mesa*, p. 234) *Diálogo II, ¿Te gusta la sopa?*, p. 236 Activities 19-21, p. 236 *Cultura viva*, p. 237 Activity 22, p. 237 *Estructura*, p. 238 Activities 23-26, pp. 239-240	Quiz Activities 2-4 CD: *Diálogo II, ¿Te gusta la sopa?* (Track 11) CD: Activities 19-21 (Tracks 12-14) CD: *Cultura viva, Las arepas venezolanas* (Track 15) CD: Activity 22 (Track 16) CD: Activity 24 (Track 17) Listening Activity 6 (Track 6) Workbook Activities 12-15 Grammar and Vocabulary Activity 13

Notes

Textbook *(Lecciones A y B)*	**Support Materials**
Warm-up: Review dialog, culture and using demonstrative adjectives (*Diálogo II, ¿Te gusta la sopa?*, p. 236; *Cultura viva*, p. 237; *Estructura*, p. 238)	Quiz Activities 5-6
	CD: *Lectura cultural, Una deliciosa tradición* (Track 18)
	Activity 30 (Track 19)
Activities 27-28, pp. 240-241	Workbook Activity 16
¡Extra!, p. 241	Communicative Activities (Information Gap
Lectura cultural, Una deliciosa tradición, p. 242	Activities/Postcard Activities/*Funciones de Comunicación*)
Activities 29-30, p. 242	CD: *Vocabulario I, La casa de Julián* (Track 1)
Autoevaluación, p. 243	Transparencies 44-45
Palabras y expresiones, p. 243	CD: Activity 1 (Track 2)
Vocabulario I, La casa de Julián, p. 244	
Activities 1-2, p. 245	
¡Extra!, p. 245	

Notes

Warm-up: Review *Autoevaluación*, p. 243,
  and vocabulary (*Vocabulario I, La casa de
  Julián*, p. 244)
Activities 3-4, p. 245
Diálogo I, La casa de Elisa, p. 246
Activities 5-7, p. 246
Cultura viva, p. 247
Activities 8-9, p. 247
Estructura, p. 248
Activities 10-12, pp. 248-249

CD: Activity 3 (Track 3)
Listening Activity 1 (Track 7)
Workbook Activities 1-3
Grammar and Vocabulary Activities 1-4
Quiz Activity 1
CD: *Diálogo I, La casa de Elisa* (Track 4)
CD: Activities 5-8 (Tracks 5-8)
Listening Activity 2 (Track 8)
Workbook Activity 4
CD: Activity 10 (Track 9)
Listening Activities 3-4 (Tracks 9-10)
Workbook Activities 5-7
Grammar and Vocabulary Activity 5

Notes

Textbook *(Lección B)*	**Support Materials**

Warm-up: Review dialog, culture and telling what someone says: *decir* (*Diálogo I, La casa de Elisa*, p. 244; *Cultura viva*, p. 247; *Estructura*, p. 248)

Estructura, p. 250

Activities 13-17, pp. 250-251

Estrategia, p. 251

Vocabulario II, Un día en casa, pp. 252-253

Activities 18-19, p. 253

Diálogo II, Tengo mucho calor, p. 254

Activities 20-22, p. 254

Cultura viva, p. 255

Activities 23-24, p. 255

Repaso rápido, p. 256

Activity 25, p. 256

Quiz Activity 2

Grammar and Vocabulary Activity 6

CD: *Vocabulario II, Un día en casa* (Track 10)

Transparency 46

CD: Activities 18-19 (Tracks 11-12)

Listening Activity 5 (Track 11)

Workbook Activities 8-10

Grammar and Vocabulary Activities 7-8

CD: *Diálogo II, Tengo mucho calor* (Track 13)

CD: Activities 20-22 (Tracks 14-16)

Notes

Warm-up: Review expressing wishes with *querer* and *gustaría,* vocabulary, dialog and culture (*Estructura*, p. 250; *Vocabulario II, Un día en casa*, pp. 252-253; *Diálogo II, Tengo mucho calor*, p. 254; *Cultura viva*, p. 255)

Estructura, p. 257

¡Extra!, p. 257

Activities 26-32, pp. 257-259

Lectura personal, p. 260

Activities 33-34, p. 260

Autoevaluación, p. 261

Palabras y expresiones, p. 261

Quiz Activities 3-5

CD: Activity 29 (Track 17)

Listening Activities 6-7 (Tracks 12-13)

Workbook Activities 11-14

Grammar and Vocabulary Activities 9-12

CD: *Lectura personal* (Track 18)

CD: Activities 33-34 (Tracks 19-20)

Workbook Activity 15

Communicative Activities (Information Gap Activities/Postcard Activities/*Funciones de Comunicación*)

Notes

Textbook *(Lección B)*	**Support Materials**
Warm-up: Review stem-changing verbs: $e \rightarrow i$ (*Estructura*, p. 257), *Autoevaluación*, p. 261, and start review for test on *Capítulo 6*	Quiz Activity 6
	CD: *¡Viento en popa!, Tú lees, La casa de mis sueños* (Track 21)
Tú lees, La casa de mis sueños, pp. 262-263	CD: Activities A-B (Tracks 22-23)
Estrategia, p. 262	Communicative Activities (Situation Cards)
Activities A-B, p. 263	Activities for Proficiency (Activities 82-94)
Tú escribes, p. 264	CD-ROM Software, Module 2
Estrategia, p. 264	Video/DVD Program, Episode 6
Proyectos adicionales, Activities A-D, p. 265	Select an activity from *Capítulo 6* to include in the *Navegando 1* Portfolio Assessment. Suggestion: Checklist appropriate items on appendices A-J, as needed.

Notes

Warm-up: Continue review for test on
Capítulo 6 and review chosen activities
from *Tú lees*, pp. 262-263, *Tú escribes*,
p. 264, and *Proyectos adicionales*, Activities
A-D, p. 265
Repaso, p. 266
Trabalenguas, p. 266
Vocabulario, p. 267
Test on *Capítulo 6*

CD: *Trabalenguas* (Track 24)
Test Booklet
CD: Listening Comprehension Tests
(Tracks 1-5)
Select an activity from *Capítulo 6* to include
in the *Navegando 1* Portfolio Assessment.
Suggestion: Checklist appropriate items
on appendices A-J, as needed.

Notes

Capítulo 7, Lecciones A y B

Day 1 | **Textbook** *(Lección A)* | **Support Materials**

Warm-up: Review test on *Capítulo 6*
Chapter opener, pp. 268-269
Vocabulario I, Los pasatiempos, pp. 270-271
Activities 1-2, p. 271
Diálogo I, ¿No quieres jugar al ajedrez?,
   p. 272
Activities 3-5, p. 272
¡Extra!, p. 272
Cultura viva, p. 273
Activity 6, p. 273

TPR Storytelling Manual
Materiales para hispanohablantes nativos
CD: *Vocabulario I, Los pasatiempos* (Track 1)
Transparencies 47-48
CD: Activity 1 (Track 2)
Listening Activity 1 (Track 14)
Workbook Activities 1-2
Grammar and Vocabulary Activities 1-3
CD: *Diálogo I, ¿No quieres jugar al ajedrez?*
   (Track 3)
CD: Activities 3-6 (Tracks 4-7)
Listening Activity 2 (Track 15)
Workbook Activity 3

Notes

Textbook *(Lección A)*	**Support Materials**
Warm-up: Review vocabulary, dialog and culture *(Vocabulario I, Los pasatiempos,* pp. 270-271; *Diálogo I, ¿No quieres jugar al ajedrez?,* p. 272; *Cultura viva,* p. 273)	Quiz Activity 1
	CD: Activity 7 (Track 8)
	CD: Activity 9 (Track 9)
	Listening Activity 3 (Track 16)
Estructura, p. 274	Workbook Activities 4-7
Activities 7-12, pp. 274-275	Grammar and Vocabulary Activities 4-6
Vocabulario II, El tiempo libre, p. 276	CD: *Vocabulario II, El tiempo libre* (Track 10)
Activities 13-14, p. 277	Transparency 49
Diálogo II, Quiero alquilar una película, p. 278	CD: Activities 13-14 (Tracks 11-12)
Activities 15-17, p. 278	Listening Activity 4 (Track 17)
Cultura viva, p. 279	Workbook Activities 8-9
Activity 18, p. 279	Grammar and Vocabulary Activities 7-8
	CD: *Diálogo II, Quiero alquilar una película* (Track 13)
	CD: Activities 15-17 (Tracks 14-16)

Notes

Day 3

Textbook *(Lección A)*　　　　　　**Support Materials**

Warm-up: Review stem-changing verbs:
　o → *ue* and *u* → *ue*, vocabulary and
　dialog (*Estructura*, p. 274; *Vocabulario II,*
　El tiempo libre, p. 276; *Diálogo II, Quiero*
　alquilar una película, p. 278)
Estructura, p. 280
Activities 19-21, pp. 280-281
¡Extra!, p. 281
Estructura, p. 282
Activities 22-24, pp. 282-283
Activities 25-26, p. 284
Estrategia, p. 284
Repaso rápido, p. 284

Quiz Activities 2-3
CD: Activities 19-20 (Tracks 17-18)
Listening Activity 5 (Track 18)
Workbook Activities 10-11
Grammar and Vocabulary Activities 9-10
CD: Activity 22 (Track 19)
Listening Activities 6-7 (Tracks 19-20)
Workbook Activity 12
Grammar and Vocabulary Activities 11-13

Notes

Textbook *(Lecciones A y B)*	**Support Materials**
Warm-up: Review culture, expressions with hace and saying what is happening: present progressive (*Cultura viva,* p. 279; *Estructura,* p. 280; *Estructura,* p. 282)	Quiz Activity 4 CD: Activities 27-28 (Tracks 20-21) Workbook Activity 13 Grammar and Vocabulary Activity 14
Estructura, p. 285	CD: *Lectura cultural, El juego de pato*
Activities 27-30, pp. 285-286	(Track 22)
¡Extra!, p. 286	Activities 34-35 (Tracks 23-24)
Activities 31-33, pp. 286-287	Workbook Activity 14
Lectura cultural, El juego de pato, p. 288	Communicative Activities (Information Gap
Activities 34-35, p. 288	Activities/Postcard Activities/*Funciones de*
Autoevaluación, p. 289	*Comunicación)*
Palabras y expresiones, p. 289	

Notes

Day 5

Textbook *(Lección B)*   **Support Materials**

Warm-up: Review using the present
  progressive with direct object pronouns
  (*Estructura,* p. 285) and *Autoevaluación,*
  p. 289
Vocabulario I, Las estaciones en Chile,
  pp. 290-291
Activities 1-2, p. 291
¡Extra!, p. 291
Diálogo I, ¡Vamos a esquiar!, p. 292
Activities 3-5, p. 292
Cultura viva, p. 293
Activity 6-7, p. 293
Estructura, p. 294
Activities 8-10, pp. 294-295

Quiz Activities 5-6
CD: *Vocabulario I, Las estaciones en Chile*
  (Track 1)
Transparency 50
CD: Activities 1-2 (Tracks 2-3)
Listening Activity 1 (Track 21)
Workbook Activities 1-3
Grammar and Vocabulary Activities 1-2
CD: *Diálogo I, ¡Vamos a esquiar!* (Track 4)
CD: Activities 3-6 (Tracks 5-8)
Listening Activity 2 (Track 22)
Workbook Activity 4-6
Grammar and Vocabulary Activity 3

Notes

| **Day 6** | **Textbook** (*Lección B*) | **Support Materials** |

Warm-up: Review vocabulary, dialog,
  culture and verbs that require special
  accentuation (*Vocabulario I, Las estaciones
  en Chile*, pp. 290-291; *Diálogo I, ¡Vamos
  a esquiar!*, p. 292; *Cultura viva*, p. 293;
  Estructura, p. 294)
Estructura, p. 296
Activities 11-15, pp. 296-297
Vocabulario II, El tiempo, pp. 298-299
Activities 16-18, p. 299
Diálogo II, ¿Qué temperatura hace?, p. 300
Activities 19-21, p. 300
Cultura viva, p. 301
Activities 22-23, p. 301

Quiz Activities 1-2
CD: Activity 11 (Track 9)
Listening Activity 3 (Track 23)
Workbook Activities 7-8
Grammar and Vocabulary Activities 4-5
CD: Activity 14 (Track 10)
CD: *Vocabulario II, El tiempo* (Track 11)
Transparencies 51-52
CD: Activities 16-17 (Tracks 12-13)
Listening Activity 4 (Track 24)
Workbook Activities 9-11
Grammar and Vocabulary Activities 6-9
CD: *Diálogo II, ¿Qué temperatura hace?*
  (Track 14)
CD: Activities 19-21 (Tracks 15-17)

Notes

Textbook *(Lección B)*	**Support Materials**
Warm-up: Review present tense of *dar* and *poner,* vocabulary, dialog and culture (*Estructura,* p. 296; *Vocabulario II, El tiempo,* pp. 298-299; *Diálogo II, ¿Qué temperatura hace?,* p. 300; *Cultura viva,* p. 301)	Quiz Activities 3-5
	CD: Activity 24 (Track 18)
	Listening Activity 5 (Track 25)
	Workbook Activity 12
	Grammar and Vocabulary Activity 10
	CD: Activity 27 (Track 19)
Estructura, p. 302	Listening Activity 6 (Track 26)
Activities 24-26, pp. 302-303	Workbook Activities 13-15
¡Oportunidades!, p. 303	Grammar and Vocabulary Activities 11-12
Estructura, p. 304	CD: *Lectura personal* (Track 20)
Activities 27-31, pp. 304-307	CD: Activities 32-33 (Tracks 21-22)
Lectura personal, p. 308	Workbook Activity 16
Activities 32-33, p. 308	Communicative Activities (Information Gap Activities/Postcard Activities/*Funciones de Comunicación*)
Autoevaluación, p. 309	
Palabras y expresiones, p. 309	

Notes

Warm-up: Review describing people using
   -dar and *-ista* (*Estructura,* p. 302), using
   ordinal numbers (*Estructura,* p. 304),
   Autoevaluación, p. 309, and start review
   for test on *Capítulo 7*
Tú lees, El mundo de los deportes,
   pp. 310-311
Estrategia, p. 310
Activities A-B, p. 311
Tú escribes, p. 312
Estrategia, p. 312
Proyectos adicionales, Activities A-C, p. 313

Quiz Activity 6
CD: *¡Viento en popa!, Tú lees, El mundo de los deportes* (Track 23)
CD: Activities A-B (Tracks 24-25)
Communicative Activities (Situation Cards)
Activities for Proficiency (Activities 95-102)
CD-ROM Software, Module 3
Video/DVD Program, Episode 7
Select an activity from *Capítulo 7* to include
   in the *Navegando 1* Portfolio Assessment.
   Suggestion: Checklist appropriate items
   on appendices A-J, as needed.

Notes

Textbook *(Lección B)*

Support Materials

Warm-up: Continue review for test on
  Capítulo 7 and review chosen activities
  from *Tú lees,* pp. 310-311, *Tú escribes,*
  p. 312, and *Proyectos adicionales,* p. 313
Repaso, p. 314
Trabalenguas, p. 314
Vocabulario, p. 315
Test on *Capítulo 7*

CD: *Trabalenguas* (Track 26)
Test Booklet
CD: Listening Comprehension Tests
  (Tracks 6-10)
Select an activity from *Capítulo 7* to include
  in the *Navegando 1* Portfolio Assessment.
  Suggestion: Checklist appropriate items
  on appendices A-J, as needed.

Notes

Capítulo 8, Lecciones A y B

Day 1	**Textbook** (*Lección A*)	**Support Materials**

Warm-up: Review test on *Capítulo 7*
Chapter opener, pp. 316-317
Vocabulario I, Los quehaceres, pp. 318-319
Activities 1-3, p. 319
Estrategia, p. 319
Diálogo I, ¿Me ayudas?, p. 320
Activities 4-6, p. 320
Cultura viva, p. 321
Activity 7, p. 321
Repaso rápido, p. 322
Activity 8, p. 322
¡Extra!, p. 322

TPR Storytelling Manual
Materiales para hispanohablantes nativos
CD: *Vocabulario I, Los quehaceres* (Track 1)
Transparencies 53-54
CD: Activities 1-2 (Tracks 2-3)
Listening Activity 1 (Track 27)
Workbook Activity 1
Grammar and Vocabulary Activities 1-2
CD: *Diálogo I, ¿Me ayudas?* (Track 4)
CD: Activities 4-6 (Tracks 5-7)
Listening Activity 2 (Track 28)
Workbook Activities 2-3
CD: Activity 8 (Track 8)
Grammar and Vocabulary Activity 3

Notes

Warm-up: Review vocabulary, dialog, culture and direct object pronouns (*Vocabulario I, Los quehaceres*, pp. 318-319; *Diálogo I, ¿Me ayudas?*, p. 320; *Cultura viva*, p. 321; *Repaso rápido*, p. 322)

Estructura, p. 323

¡Extra!, p. 324

Activities 9-15, pp. 324-326

Estructura, p. 326

Activities 16-18, pp. 326-327

¡Oportunidades!, p. 327

Vocabulario II, Más quehaceres, pp. 328-329

Activities 19-20, p. 329

Diálogo II, Hay mucho por hacer, p. 330

Activity 21, p. 330

Quiz Activity 1

CD: Activities 10-11 (Tracks 9-10)

Listening Activities 3-4 (Tracks 29-30)

Workbook Activities 4-6

Grammar and Vocabulary Activities 4-7

CD: Activities 16-17 (Tracks 11-12)

Listening Activity 5 (Track 31)

Workbook Activity 7

Grammar and Vocabulary Activity 8

CD: *Vocabulario II, Más quehaceres* (Track 13)

Transparencies 55-56

CD: Activity 19 (Track 14)

Grammar and Vocabulary Activities 9-10

Listening Activity 6 (Track 32)

Workbook Activity 8

CD: *Diálogo II, Hay mucho por hacer* (Track 15)

CD: Activity 21 (Track 16)

Notes

| **Day 3** | **Textbook** *(Lección A)* | **Support Materials** |

Warm-up: Review indirect object pronouns, saying what just happened with *acabar de*, vocabulary and dialog (*Estructura*, p. 323; *Estructura*, p. 326; *Vocabulario II, Más quehaceres*, pp. 328-329; *Diálogo II, Hay mucho por hacer*, p. 330)

Activities 22-23, p. 330

¡Extra!, p. 330

Cultura viva, p. 331

Activities 24-25, p. 331

Estructura, p. 332

Activities 26-28, pp. 332-333

Estructura, p. 334

Activities 29-31, pp. 334-335

CD: Activities 22-24 (Tracks 17-19)
Quiz Activities 2-3
Listening Activity 7 (Track 33)
Workbook Activities 9-10
Grammar and Vocabulary Activities 11-12
CD: Activity 31 (Track 20)
Listening Activity 8 (Track 34)
Workbook Activity 11
Grammar and Vocabulary Activity 13

Notes

Day 4

Textbook *(Lecciones A y B)*

Support Materials

Warm-up: Review culture, present tense of *oír* and *traer* and talking about the past: preterite tense of *-ar* verbs (*Cultura viva*, p. 331; *Estructura*, p. 332; *Estructura*, p. 334)

Activities 32-33, p. 335

Lectura cultural, ¿Quién lo hace?, p. 336

Activities 34-35, p. 336

Autoevaluación, p. 337

Palabras y expresiones, p. 337

Vocabulario I, El supermercado, p. 338

Activities 1-2, p. 339

¡Extra!, p. 339

Quiz Activities 4-6

CD: *Lectura cultural, ¿Quién lo hace?* (Track 22)

Activities 34-35 (Tracks 22-23)

Workbook Activity 12

Communicative Activities (Information Gap Activities/Postcard Activities/*Funciones de Comunicación*)

CD: *Vocabulario I, El supermercado* (Track 1)

Transparencies 57-58

CD: Activity 1 (Track 2)

Listening Activity 1 (Track 35)

Workbook Activities 1-2

Grammar and Vocabulary Activities 1-5

Notes

| **Day 5** | **Textbook** (*Lección B*) | **Support Materials** |

Warm-up: Review *Autoevaluación*, p. 337,
and vocabulary (*Vocabulario I, El
supermercado*, p. 338)
Diálogo I, ¿Qué nos hace falta comprar?, p. 340
Activities 3-5, p. 340
Cultura viva, p. 341
Activities 6-8, p. 341
¡Extra!, p. 341
Estructura, pp. 342-343
Activities 9-19, pp. 343-347

Quiz Activity 1
CD: *Diálogo I, ¿Qué nos hace falta comprar?*
(Track 3)
CD: Activities 3-6 (Tracks 4-6)
CD: *Cultura viva, La paella* (Track 7)
CD: Activity 6 (Track 8)
Listening Activity 2 (Track 36)
CD: Activity 10 (Track 9)
CD: Activity 12 (Track 10)
CD: Activity 15 (Track 11)
Listening Activities 3-5 (Tracks 37-39)
Workbook Activities 3-6
Grammar and Vocabulary Activities 6-10

Notes

Textbook *(Lección B)*	**Support Materials**
Warm-up: Review dialog, culture and making comparisons (*Diálogo I, ¿Qué nos hace falta comprar?*, p. 340; *Cultura viva*, p. 341; *Estructura*, pp. 342-343)	Quiz Activity 2
	CD: *Vocabulario II, El mercado* (Track 12)
	Transparencies 59-60
Vocabulario II, El mercado, pp. 348-349	CD: Activities 20-21 (Tracks 13-14)
Activities 20-22, p. 349	Listening Activity 6 (Track 40)
Diálogo II, Comprando chorizo, p. 350	Workbook Activities 7-8
Activities 23-25, p. 350	Grammar and Vocabulary Activities 11-13
¡Extra!, p. 350	Quiz Activity 3
Cultura viva, p. 351	CD: *Diálogo II, Comprando chorizo* (Track 15)
Activity 26, p. 351	CD: Activities 23-25 (Tracks 16-18)
Repaso rápido, p. 352	Workbook Activity 9
Activity 27, p. 352	CD: Activity 27 (Track 19)

Notes

Textbook *(Lección B)*	**Support Materials**
Warm-up: Review vocabulary, dialog, culture and preterite tense of regular *-ar* verbs (*Vocabulario II, El mercado*, pp. 348-349; *Diálogo II, Comprando chorizo*, p. 350; *Cultura viva*, p. 351; *Estructura*, p. 352)	Quiz Activity 4
	CD: Activity 29 (Track 20)
	Listening Activity 7 (Track 41)
	Workbook Activities 10-12
	Grammar and Vocabulary Activities 14-15
Estructura, p. 352	CD: *Lectura personal* (Track 21)
Activities 28-32, pp. 352-353	CD: Activities 33-34 (Tracks 22-23)
Lectura personal, p. 354	Workbook Activity 13
Activities 33-34, p. 354	Communicative Activities (Information Gap
Autoevaluación, p. 355	Activities/Postcard Activities/*Funciones de*
Palabras y expresiones, p. 355	*Comunicación*)

Notes

Textbook *(Lección B)*   **Support Materials**

Warm-up: Review preterite tense of *dar* and *estar* (*Estructura,* p. 352), *Autoevaluación,* p. 355, and start review for test on *Capítulo 8*

Tú lees, Ir de tapas y a merendar, pp. 356-357

Estrategia, p. 356

Activities A-B, p. 357

Tú escribes, Activities A-B, p. 358

Estrategia, p. 358

Proyectos adicionales, Activities A-C, p. 359

Quiz Activity 5

CD: *¡Viento en popa!, Tú lees, Ir de tapas y a merendar* (Track 24)

CD: Activities A-B (Tracks 25-26)

Communicative Activities (Situation Cards)

Activities for Proficiency (Activities 103-114)

CD-ROM Software, Module 3

Video/DVD Program, Episode 8

Select an activity from *Capítulo 8* to include in the *Navegando 1* Portfolio Assessment. Suggestion: Checklist appropriate items on appendices A-J, as needed.

Notes

Textbook (*Lección B*)	**Support Materials**

Warm-up: Continue review for test on *Capítulo 8* and review chosen activities from *Tú lees*, pp. 356-357, *Tú escribes*, p. 358, and *Proyectos adicionales*, p. 359.

Repaso, p. 360

Trabalenguas, p. 360

Vocabulario, p. 361

Test on *Capítulo 8*

CD: *Trabalenguas* (Track 27)

Test Booklet

CD: Listening Comprehension Tests (Tracks 11-16)

Select an activity from *Capítulo 8* to include in the *Navegando 1* Portfolio Assessment. Suggestion: Checklist appropriate items on appendices A-J, as needed.

Notes

Capítulo 9, Lecciones A y B

Day 1

Textbook *(Lección A)*	**Support Materials**

Warm-up: Review test on *Capítulo 8*
Chapter opener, pp. 362-363
Vocabulario I, En la tienda por departamentos, pp. 364-365
Activities 1-3, p. 365
Diálogo I, ¿Cuál prefieres?, p. 366
Activities 4-6, p. 366
¡Extra!, p. 366
Cultura viva, p. 367
Activities 7-8, p. 367

TPR Storytelling Manual
Materiales para hispanohablantes nativos
CD: *Vocabulario I, En la tienda por departamentos* (Track 1)
Transparencies 61-62
CD: Activity 1 (Track 2)
Listening Activity 1 (Track 1)
Workbook Activities 1-3
Grammar and Vocabulary Activities 1-4
CD: *Diálogo I, ¿Cuál prefieres?* (Track 3)
CD: Activities 4-7 (Tracks 4-7)
Listening Activity 2 (Track 2)
Workbook Activity 4

Notes

Textbook (*Lección A*)	**Support Materials**
Warm-up: Review vocabulary, dialog and culture (*Vocabulario I, En la tienda por departamentos*, pp. 364-365; *Diálogo I, ¿Cuál prefieres?*, p. 366; *Cultura viva*, p. 367) *Estructura*, p. 368 Activities 9-12, pp. 368-369 *Estrategia*, p. 369 *¡Oportunidades!*, p. 369 Activities 13-14, p. 370 *Estructura*, p. 370 Activities 15-19, pp. 371-373	Quiz Activities 1-2 Listening Activity 3 (Track 3) Workbook Activity 5 Grammar and Vocabulary Activity 5 CD: Activity 16 (Track 8) Listening Activity 4 (Track 4) Workbook Activities 6-8 Grammar and Vocabulary Activities 6-8

Notes

Textbook *(Lección A)*	**Support Materials**
Warm-up: Review adjectives as nouns and talking about the past: preterite tense of *-er* and *-ir* verbs (*Estructura*, p. 368; *Estructura*, p. 370)	Quiz Activities 3-4
	CD: *Vocabulario II, Artículos para todos* (Track 9)
	Transparency 63
Vocabulario II, Artículos para todos, pp. 374-375	CD: Activity 20 (Track 10)
Activities 20-22, p. 375	Listening Activity 5 (Track 5)
Diálogo II, Un vestido de seda, p. 376	Workbook Activity 9
Activities 23-25, p. 376	Grammar and Vocabulary Activity 9
Cultura viva, p. 377	CD: *Diálogo II, Un vestido de seda* (Track 11)
Activity 26, p. 377	CD: Activities 23-25 (Tracks 12-14)
Estructura, p. 378	CD: Activity 27 (Track 15)
Activities 27-31, pp. 379-380	Listening Activity 6 (Track 6)
	Workbook Activities 10-11
	Grammar and Vocabulary Activities 10-12

Notes

Textbook *(Lección A)*	**Support Materials**
Warm-up: Review vocabulary, dialog, culture and preterite tense of *ir* and *ser* (*Vocabulario II, Artículos para todos*, pp. 374-375; *Diálogo II, Un vestido de seda*, p. 376; *Cultura viva*, p. 377; *Estructura*, p. 378) *Estructura*, pp. 381-382 Activities 32-36, pp. 382-383 *Lectura cultural, Las molas: símbolo de la cultura kuna*, p. 384 Activities 37-38, p. 384 *Autoevaluación*, p. 385 *Palabras y expresiones*, p. 385	Quiz Activities 5-6 CD: Activities 33-34 (Tracks 16-17) Listening Activities 7-8 (Tracks 7-8) Workbook Activities 12-13 Grammar and Vocabulary Activities 13-14 CD: *Lectura cultural, Las molas: símbolo de la cultura kuna* (Track 18) Activity 37 (Track 19) Workbook Activity 14 Communicative Activities (Information Gap Activities/Postcard Activities/*Funciones de Comunicación*)

Notes

Warm-up: Review affirmative and negative
words (*Estructura,* pp. 381-382) and
Autoevaluación, p. 385
Vocabulario I, Regalos, pp. 386-387
Activities 1-3, p. 387
Diálogo I, Busco un regalo, p. 388
Activities 4-6, p. 388
¡Extra!, p. 388
Cultura viva, p. 389
Activity 7, p. 389
Estructura, p. 390
Activities 8-10, p. 390

Quiz Activity 7
CD: *Vocabulario I, Regalos* (Track 1)
Transparencies 64-65
CD: Activity 1 (Track 2)
Listening Activity 1 (Track 9)
Workbook Activities 1-3
Grammar and Vocabulary Activities 1-3
CD: *Diálogo I, Busco un regalo* (Track 3)
CD: Activities 4-6 (Tracks 4-6)
Listening Activity 2 (Track 10)
Workbook Activity 4
CD: Activities 8-9 (Tracks 7-8)
Listening Activity 3 (Track 11)
Workbook Activity 5
Grammar and Vocabulary Activity 4

Notes

Textbook (*Lección B*)	**Support Materials**
Warm-up: Review vocabulary, dialog, culture and diminutives (*Vocabulario I, Regalos,* pp. 386-387; *Diálogo I, Busco un regalo,* p. 388; *Cultura viva,* p. 389; *Estructura,* p. 390)	Quiz Activity 1
	CD: Activities 12-13 (Tracks 9-10)
	Listening Activity 4 (Track 12)
	Workbook Activities 6-10
	Grammar and Vocabulary Activities 5-8
Estructura, p. 391	CD: *Vocabulario II, En la caja* (Track 11)
Activities 11-17, pp. 391-393	Transparency 66
Vocabulario II, En la caja, p. 394	CD: Activity 18 (Track 12)
Activities 18-19, p. 395	Listening Activities 5-6 (Tracks 13-14)
Diálogo II, ¿Cómo va a pagar?, p. 396	Workbook Activities 11-12
Activities 20-22, p. 396	Grammar and Vocabulary Activities 9-10
Cultura viva, p. 397	CD: *Diálogo II, ¿Cómo va a pagar?* (Track 13)
Activity 23, p. 397	CD: Activities 20-22 (Tracks 14-16)
Repaso rápido, p. 398	CD: *Cultura viva, De compras en Guayaquil* (Track 17)
Activity 24, p. 398	

Notes

Warm-up: Review preterite tense of *leer*, *oír*, *ver*, *decir*, *hacer* and *tener*, vocabulary, dialog and culture (*Estructura*, p. 391; *Vocabulario II, En la caja*, p. 394; *Diálogo II, ¿Cómo va a pagar?*, p. 396; *Cultura viva*, p. 397)	Quiz Activities 2-5
	CD: Activity 26 (Track 18)
	Listening Activity 7 (Track 15)
	Workbook Activity 13
	Grammar and Vocabulary Activities 11-13
Estructura, pp. 398-399	CD: *Lectura personal* (Track 19)
Activities 25-31, pp. 399-401	CD: Activity 33 (Track 20)
Lectura personal, p. 402	Workbook Activity 14
Activities 32-33, p. 402	Communicative Activities (Information
Autoevaluación, p. 403	Gap Activities/Postcard
Palabras y expresiones, p. 403	Activities/*Funciones de Comunicación*)

Notes

Warm-up: Review prepositions and using prepositions *(Repaso rápido,* p. 398; *Estructura,* pp. 398-399), *Autoevaluación,* p. 403, and start review for test on *Capítulo 9*

Tú lees, Las rebajas de Danté, p. 404

Estrategia, p. 404

Activities A-B, p. 405

Tú escribes, p. 406

Estrategia, p. 406

Proyectos adicionales, Activities A-C, p. 407

Quiz Activity 6

CD: *¡Viento en popa!, Tú lees, Las rebajas de Danté* (Track 21)

CD: Activities A-B (Tracks 22-23)

Communicative Activities (Situation Cards)

Activities for Proficiency (Activities 115-124)

CD-ROM Software, Module 4

Video/DVD Program, Episode 9

Select an activity from *Capítulo 9* to include in the *Navegando 1* Portfolio Assessment. Suggestion: Checklist appropriate items on appendices A-J, as needed.

Notes

Textbook *(Lección B)*   **Support Materials**

Warm-up: Continue review for test on *Capítulo 9* and review chosen activities from *Tú lees*, p. 404, *Tú escribes*, p. 406, and *Proyectos adicionales*, p. 407

Repaso, p. 408

Trabalenguas, p. 408

Vocabulario, p. 409

Test on *Capítulo 9*

CD: *Trabalenguas* (Track 24)

Test Booklet

CD: Listening Comprehension Tests (Tracks 17-21)

Select an activity from *Capítulo 9* to include in the *Navegando 1* Portfolio Assessment. Suggestion: Checklist appropriate items on appendices A-J, as needed.

Notes

Capítulo 10, Lecciones A y B

<table>
<tr><td>**Day 1**</td><td>**Textbook** (*Lección A*)</td><td>**Support Materials**</td></tr>
</table>

Textbook (*Lección A*)	Support Materials
Warm-up: Review test on *Capítulo 9*	TPR Storytelling Manual
Chapter opener, pp. 410-411	*Materiales para hispanohablantes nativos*
Diálogo I, Fue un año divertido, p. 412	CD: *Diálogo I, Fue un año divertido* (Track 1)
Activities 1-3, p. 412	Transparency 67
Cultura viva, p. 413	CD: Activities 1-4 (Tracks 2-5)
Activities 4-5, p. 413	Listening Activities 1-3 (Tracks 16-18)
¡Oportunidades!, p. 413	Workbook Activities 1-4
	Grammar and Vocabulary Activity 1

Notes

Day 2

Textbook *(Lección A)*	**Support Materials**

Warm-up: Review dialog and culture
   (*Diálogo I, Fue un año divertido*, p. 412;
   Cultura viva, p. 413)
Estrategia, p. 414
Activities 6-11, pp. 414-415

Quiz Activities 1-2
Listening Activity 4 (Track 19)
Workbook Activities 5-9
Grammar and Vocabulary Activities 2-6

Notes

Textbook *(Lecciones A y B)*	**Support Materials**
Warm-up: Review work on Activities 6-11, pp. 414-415	Quiz Activity 3
Lectura cultural, Machu Picchu, p. 416	CD: *Lectura cultural, Machu Picchu* (Track 6)
Activities 12-13, p. 416	CD: Activities 12-13 (Tracks 7-8)
Autoevaluación, p. 417	Workbook Activity 10
Diálogo I, ¿Adónde van de vacaciones?, p. 418	Communicative Activities (Information Gap Activities/Postcard Activities/*Funciones de Comunicación*)
Activity 1, p. 418	

Notes

Textbook *(Lección B)*   **Support Materials**

Warm-up: Review *Autoevaluación*, p. 417,   Quiz Activities 4-5
   and dialog (*Diálogo I, ¿Adónde van de*   CD: *Diálogo I, ¿Adónde van de vacaciones?*
   vacaciones?, p. 418)   (Track 1)
Activities 2-3, p. 418   Transparency 68
¡Extra!, p. 418   CD: Activities 1-4 (Tracks 2-5)
Cultura viva, p. 419   Listening Activities 1-6 (Tracks 20-25)
Activities 4-10, pp. 419-421   Workbook Activities 1-5
¡Oportunidades!, p. 421   Grammar and Vocabulary Activities 1-7

Notes

Textbook *(Lección B)*	**Support Materials**

Warm-up: Review culture (*Cultura viva*, p. 419) and Activities 5-10, pp. 420-421
Activity 11, p. 421
Lectura personal, p. 422
Activities 12-13, p. 422
Autoevaluación, p. 423
Estrategia, p. 424
Tú lees, Activities A-B, pp. 424-425

Quiz Activities 1-2
CD: *Lectura personal* (Track 6)
CD: Activities 12-13 (Tracks 7-8)
Workbook Activities 6-8
CD: *¡Viento en popa!, Tú lees, Es sólo una cuestión de actitud* (Track 9)
CD: Activity B (Track 10)
Communicative Activities (Information Gap Activities/Postcard Activities/*Funciones de Comunicación*)

Notes

Textbook *(Lección B)*	**Support Materials**
Warm-up: Review *Autoevaluación*, p. 423, and review for test on *Capítulo 10* *Tú escribes*, p. 426 *Estrategia*, p. 426 *Proyectos adicionales*, Activities A-C, p. 427 *Repaso*, p.428 *Trabalenguas*, p. 428	Quiz Activities 3-5 CD: *Trabalenguas* (Track 11) Communicative Activities (Situation Cards) Activities for Proficiency (Activities 125-158) CD-ROM Software, Module 4 Video/DVD Program, Episode 10 Spanish Reader, *El viaje a Guatemala* Select an activity from *Capítulo 10* to include in the *Navegando 1* Portfolio Assessment. Suggestion: Checklist appropriate items on appendices A-J, as needed.

Notes

	Support Materials

Test on *Capítulo 10*

Test Booklet
CD: Listening Comprehension Tests
    (Tracks 22-25)
Select an activity from *Capítulo 10* to
    include in the *Navegando 1* Portfolio
    Assessment. Suggestion: Checklist
    appropriate items on appendices A-J,
    as needed.

Notes

Achievement Test II

Test Booklet
CD: Achievement Test II (Tracks 26-35)
Select an activity from *Capítulo 10* to
   include in the *Navegando 1* Portfolio
   Assessment. Suggestion: Checklist
   appropriate items on appendices A-J,
   as needed.

Notes